Copyright © 2020 by Deb Lilith

All rights reserved.

No part of this book may be reproduced in any form or by any electronic or mechanical means, including information storage and retrieval systems, without written permission from the author, except for the use of brief quotations in a book review.

❦ Created with Vellum

CONTENTS

CHAKRAS FOR BEGINNERS

Introduction	3
1. What Are Chakras	5
2. Developing Your Chakras	24
3. Keeping Your Chakras Balanced	30
4. Myths About Chakras	46
5. Improving Your Chakra Healing Process	53
6. Common Risks to Opening Chakras	57
7. Mistakes Made When Opening Chakras	63
8. Techniques to Heal Chakras	68
9. What Could Be Slowing You Down	121
10. Opening The Third Eye	125
11. Commonly Asked Questions	132
Conclusion	135

BUDDHISM

Introduction	139
1. The Origins of Buddhism	141
2. Buddhist Teachings and Principles	158
3. Buddhism Numbers	181
4. Buddhist Perfections	211
5. Karma	225
6. Rebirth	236
7. Bringing Buddhism Into Your Life	248
Conclusion	267

5 ESSENTIAL MINDFUL HABITS

Introduction	271
1. What is Mindfulness?	273

2. Mindful Eating	278
3. Mindful Breathing	283
4. Expressing Gratitude	288
5. Conscious Observation	294
6. Mindful Meditation	297
Conclusion	305

CHAKRAS
FOR BEGINNERS
A Complete Guide to Chakra Healing

DEB LILITH

Copyright © 2020 by Deb Lilith

All rights reserved.

No part of this book may be reproduced in any form or by any electronic or mechanical means, including information storage and retrieval systems, without written permission from the author, except for the use of brief quotations in a book review.

INTRODUCTION

Congratulations, and thank you for choosing this book about chakras. I hope that you find the information helpful and informative. Throughout this book, we will be discussing the chakras, how they affect you, and how you can open them.

To truly be wise, one has to learn from the mistakes that other people make. Books are created as a way to provide people with greater knowledge so that their life can become better in the long run. Great books have the ability to create a path that wasn't originally there, opening ways to great things.

This book aims to clear a path for you to reach an understanding of the chakra system and how they control your bodily energy. It's unfortunate that the majority of people walk around with blocked chakras because of things they have experienced in their life. The great thing is that chakras can be healed. The process of healing chakras requires practice and learning.

This can all be helped by switching up how you have been doing things. When we become aware of the smaller parts of our life, it

INTRODUCTION

will bring us to new healing levels. As you read through this book, you will discover meditations and exercises that will help you to heal your chakras. As you learn more about yourself, make sure that you fully take in the information. As you begin to work towards making your life more fulfilling, you will likely find a better sense of what your purpose is.

The goal of this book is to bring you more joy. Your way of looking at life will grow, and it will transform the negativity within your life into something that can help you reach your higher purpose. It's important that you enjoy this process and be thankful for all of the energy that you can use.

There are plenty of other books on this subject on the market, thanks once more for choosing this one! Every effort was made to ensure it is full of as much useful information as possible; please enjoy!

WHAT ARE CHAKRAS

NOT EVERYONE IS familiar with the chakras, but they are being talked about more and more. People who believe in holistic practices, Reiki healings, meditations, and yoga believe in chakras. It isn't just all hoo-doo. Even though western research isn't abundant, it has been said that the chakra system began in India between the years of 1500 and 500 BC in the oldest text known as the *Vedas*.

This is just my opinion, but to me, it only takes one session of learning your energy system to know that chakras are indeed real, and they resonate with you every second of every day.

The best description I can give you about chakras is they are energy wheels. Chakra, in Sanskrit, means wheel, round, or a tunnel where energy exchanges take place. Therefore, chakra could mean a circular movement where bad energy gets exchanged for good. Basically, bad energy goes out; good energy comes in. This energy is known as Prana or the vital life force. This is what keeps us healthy, alive, and vibrant. Each chakra will correspond with a major organ and the nerve centers in our bodies. Every one of the seven main chakras contains our emotional and spiritual states.

Life and time have been thought actually to be controlled by the chakras. Because of this, chakras are seen as colored wheels of light that spin at various speeds and intensity. To put it simply, chakras are the centers that receive, absorb, and transmit energies.

Chakras are a point that exists between the non-physical and physical realms of the human body. The energy that gets exchanged in the chakras is the energy of the life force. This is the reason we study chakras and need to know how they work.

If your chakras are blocked, this means you can't function properly either physically, psychologically, or mentally. When your chakras are blocked, there isn't any energy exchange, and this isn't good. Think about it like a car's exhaust system. If the exhaust is blocked, the car is going to choke out and stall.

Our bodies experience pretty much the same thing if your chakras are blocked. All this bad energy gets kept inside. If this exchange can't take place, bad things like illness will begin to affect your body. No one wants this to happen. Our goal needs to be that every chakra remains open and aligned with all the energy flowing freely between all of them while keeping them connected. If there is a blockage in just one, the energy won't be able to flow through the body and will create some stagnant energy that, with time, is going to manifest certain physical and emotional imbalances.

Your chakras can also be unbalanced. This happens when negative energy outweighs the positive. Basically, inside your body, the bad overcomes the good. Keeping the energy freely flowing in our bodies while keeping the chakras open and balanced is a lot easier if we can be aware of them and what imbalances could feel like. Just being able to balance on will help bring all the others into balance, too.

Having unbalanced chakras isn't all about the negative exceeding the positive. If certain chakras like the crown chakra are unbalanced, you might be spending too much time pursuing spirituality and aren't taking enough time to take care of your physical self. If this is the case, you need to ground yourself.

Since chakras can become blocked, they can also be unblocked. This means you can reverse the damage and actually enjoy your life. Many things need to happen to unblock and balance the chakras. The main ones would be using various types of yoga, meditating, therapy, and others. We will look at these in more detail later on.

Our bodies have many chakras, the ones that are recognized the most are the seven that are located along the spine. They work to control certain aspects of your health.

There have been many maps created to show the chakra system. There are thousands of points and channels along with side and major central channels. Just think about acupuncture and the meridian lines. Some people say that there might be as many as 114 chakra points. This number includes chakras that are found below and above our physical bodies that are known as the astral and subtle body.

*L*et me give you the history of chakras and then a quick insight as to why you need to work with them to keep them healthy and their energy flowing freely.

A QUICK HISTORY

Many cultures have practiced the concept of chakras for many thousands of years, but by different names. Any religion or culture that encourages meditation is doing some form of chakra. Meditation is encouraged with chakras as a way of listening to our inner self and tapping into our subconscious, but it is a way to balance any unbalanced chakras.

*T*he psychology of chakras is now a common practice. There are a lot of people who live in the West that are practicing this as well as ayurvedic and Chinese medicine systems. The best thing about this is you don't need a trainer to unblock and balance your chakras. You do have to put in place some precautionary and safety measures.

. . .

While it isn't as well established in the West as it is in other parts of the world like India, people are beginning to realize the benefits of mental and emotional health, self-awareness, and spirituality. Many people all over the world are beginning to practice it every day.

The concept of chakras has a long lineage that is linked to complicated spiritual practices. The most dominant spiritual tradition that used chakras started in India, as shown by Yogic and Tantric traditions of Buddhism and Hinduism.

In the 800s BC, Yogic teachings said a vital force called Prana flowed through pathways that are called nadis. These pathways were believed to work in the junction points like chakras.

Chakra practices have been shown in the Jewish religion and hesychastic traditions. Hesychastic tradition uses a meditation that has similar features to yogic and tantric traditions. Jewish religions believe in divine qualities and psychic powers that can be found in the body.

Chakra practices were brought to the United States and Europe by Englishman John Woodroffe. While working as a lawyer in India, he brought scriptures from Hindu that described chakras.

. . .

English books called *Nuclear Evolution*, *The Book of Color Healing*, and *The Serpent Power* would come along later. These books opened many paths for chakras to come into the health systems and alternative medicine of countries of the West.

Nowadays, chakras play a huge role in diagnosing the causes of many imbalances within our bodies, psychological and mental well being in our lives. Healers and therapists have affirmed chakras in the Western psychological world. Besides using its concept within their practice, they are spreading awareness and knowledge of it.

ROOT CHAKRA – MULADHARA

The root chakra is also called Muladhara. A simple definition means "supporting your roots." This meaning comes from splitting the word Muladhara into two words: "Mula," which means root, and "Dhara," which means support.

This chakra is the first one of importance. When you balance this chakra, you are creating a solid foundation to open the remaining chakras. Just think about laying a foundation for a house that you will be living in for the rest of your life. This foundation is embedded in firm soil and will give you the stability that you need to make a home that is filled with joy for many years.

. . .

This chakra is the base for consciousness in the body. The necessity for it can be felt when the energy connects us to the earth. Therefore, it relates to material requirements, emotional needs, sexuality, physical strength, and survival. When you look at the modern world, this chakra basically translates to financial and emotional security.

It doesn't matter if you feel secure now; it has more to do with how safe you felt as a child. If you look at psychologist Erik Erickson's developmental states, the first state of trust versus mistrust is related to the development of this chakra. When you were an infant, and your caregivers gave you the things you needed to survive constantly, you should have felt secure. You thought the world was a place where your basic needs could be met. On the other hand, if your caregivers delayed or withheld giving you what you needed, you might find that your root chakra is blocked.

When looking at emotions, this chakra bases the focus on primal feelings, and the spiritual focus is based on sympathy and being able to sense energy. Its color is red and is located at the bottom of the spine.

When it is balanced, you will feel accomplishment, stability, and vibrant energy. This relates to requirements like safety, shelter, and money.

. . .

There will be times that this chakra will be unbalanced, and this gets accompanied by consequences. Excessive energy in this chakra could result in emotional instability, such as anxiety.

On the physical level, you might have prostate issues if you are a man, hip pain, lower back problems, constipation, and sluggishness. Other negative problems could show up like diarrhea and fear if this chakra doesn't get activated.

Your energy levels will also get beaten up. You will experience feelings of low self-esteem, irritability, unexplained fatigue, and daydreaming. To get this chakra balanced, the best yoga pose is the mula bandha; this is a very easy pose.

You could use the crystals of red jasper, garnet, ruby, or bloodstone to help heal and balance this chakra. You could also use the essential oils of Balance Blend, On Guard Blend, Arborvitae, Basil, Cedarwood, Vetiver, Fir, Myrrh, and Patchouli to help balance and heal this chakra.

You could say this positive affirmation to help you keep this chakra balanced: "I am a divine being of light. I am peaceful, protected, and secure."

SACRAL CHAKRA – SVADHISTHANA

A simple definition of the sacral chakra is svadhisthana. It can be broken down into two words, "sva," which means one's own, and "adhisthana," which means residence or dwelling place.

This chakra portrays the consciousness of our emotions. It relates to imagination, feelings, passions, and emotions. Its focus dwells on all our feelings. Spiritually, it allows us to express sympathy and feelings for other people's feelings.

This chakra is needed for our sexuality and creativity. It can enhance the creative energies that drive us to enjoy our lives. It motivates us to enjoy our efforts and indulge in activities that give us pleasure, like sex. This chakra's color is orange and can be found above the pubic bone and just below the navel. It surrounds the hypogastric plexus and the genital region. This chakra's element is water, and this is equivalent to cohesiveness. This chakra's energy is lunar, passive, and feminine.

Humans have an innate ability to create. Any time you garden, bake, or cook, you are creating. You create when you find new solutions to old problems. Any time you take materials, mental or physical, and turn them into new things, you are using creative energy.

The main problem with being creative is that you are discouraged from being creative, and this begins with education. After we have gone through the phase where cutting paper, painting, or coloring is acceptable, we have to mold ourselves into being less creative. We have to conform, follow all the rules, and learn to fit in. We lose our creative energy and our ideas during this process. As adults, we become used to doing what is right, the latest trends, or what other people feel is acceptable. If we are asked to invent something new, we have a hard time doing it.

Creativity, sensuality, joy, and happiness in our lives indicate this chakra is in balance. If it isn't balanced, you might suffer from restlessness, hormone imbalance, obesity, oversensitivity, and addiction. Addiction is present when a person enjoys things that can't nourish our health and soul.

If the chakra isn't active, you will have feelings of insecurity, guilt, and fear. But if we experience any under activity, we might suffer from no creative power, lack of passion, decreased sex drive, impotence, and depression.

How can we balance this chakra? There are several ways. Begin by surrounding yourself with all things orange. Wear it; put it in your office and your house. This color will soothe your feelings and trigger your creativity all at the same time. You can also try yoga poses like balasana and Nataraj asana.

You can also use the crystals like orange calcite, opal, citrine, or carnelian to help heal and balance this chakra. You could use an essential oil like Clary Calm Blend, Whisper Blend, Purify Cleansing Blend, Citrus Bliss Blend,

Cinnamon, Cypress, or Black Pepper to help balance and heal this chakra.

You can say this positive affirmation to yourself to help keep this chakra balanced: "I am authentically creating a life free from stress and full of bliss."

SOLAR PLEXUS – MANIPURA

The solar plexus chakra is also called Manipura. It can be broken down into two words, "mani," meaning jewel, and "Pura," meaning city. This chakra enhances consciousness for our mental bodies.

It can connect us to individual elements like individual expressions, self-image, our conscious minds, and personal power. Emotionally it can focus on feelings that relate to self-esteem, doubt, and fear. Spiritually it can focus on mental information and empowerment.

This chakra's responsibility is personal power and identity. It has the color yellow and is located at the navel. If it is balanced, it can enhance our feelings of self-esteem, willpower, courage, and strength.

There will be times when this chakra will either be under or overactive. If it is overactive, you will have lots of energy that can be accompanied by feelings of being hungry for power, wanting to control everything, and needing to be in control.

Being timid, feeling insecure, and indecisiveness indicates that this chakra is underactive. When this chakra isn't active or completely depleted, we are faced with chronic fatigue, poor digestion, anger problems, and powerlessness. You might be diagnosed with diabetes or hypoglycemia.

This chakra can be healed by doing the yoga pose reverse warrior or by meditating while holding a yellow stone like sunstone, yellow calcite, golden topaz, citrine, or amber. You could also use essential oils like Slim and Sassy Blend, Smart and Sassy Blend, ZenGest Blend, DigestZen, Juniper Betty, Clove, Grapefruit, Cassia, Ginger, Bergamot, or Fennel to help balance and heal this chakra. You could say this positive affirmation to yourself each day to help heal this chakra: "I am powerful, confident, and successful in all my ventures."

HEART CHAKRA – ANAHATA

The heart chakra is also called Anahata. Anahata simply means unbeaten. The name indicated that underneath all the past grievances and hurts lies a spiritual and pure place where no hurt can live. This chakra is located in the center of your chest, just above the heart. It also includes the breasts, lungs, thymus gland, and cardiac plexus. In this area, the spiritual and physical meet. If the saying "love makes the world go round" is true, then this chakra is what makes love go round.

It links our spiritual and physical aspects of life. Emotionally, this chakra focuses on feelings that are related to love and gives us a connection to the spiritually divine.

This chakra's color is green. If it is in balance, you will see that it is easy to receive and give love, being accepted, accepted, and feeling peaceful.

If this chakra is overactive, you might have negative feelings like lack of empathy, jealousy, and codependency.

Most people like to live with their grievances. They have been hurt by loved ones, classmates, siblings, or parents. You might be able to relate to this. It is totally impossible to stay away from situations where you might get hurt. Sometimes you might have thought about hurting these other people to get back at them. This isn't living in the place of Anahata. A person who inflicts pain on other people comes from places of hatred, ignorance, or fear. All of these represent a heart chakra that is closed.

If you come across feelings of hurt from either the presence of the past, you might choose to feel them, let them go, or hold onto them. If you can let them go, you will be able to open up your heart to new experiences and people with understanding, love, and compassion. Holding onto hurt shelters negative feelings and will cut you off from opportunities to serve and love others. It is easy to let go. All you have to do is make a choice to do so. Your ego and mind might try to tell you differently, but it really is as simple as just letting go and moving ahead.

. . .

There might be other negative feelings if the chakra is underactive, like intolerance, bitterness, loneliness, shyness, and blood circulation problems. To heal this chakra, you can try yoga poses Sphinx and puppy.

If you like meditating, you can surround yourself with green or go outside and enjoy all that Mother Nature is offering you. Because this chakra relates to air, it is important that you breathe in lots of fresh air and make every effort to enjoy the air. Make sure you enjoy some fresh air outside each day. It will help soothe this chakra.

You can use crystals like emerald, green aventurine, chrysocolla, rose quartz to help heal and balance this chakra. You could use an essential oil like Cardamom, Eucalyptus, Lime, Marjoram, Geranium, Peppermint, Thyme, Rose, Melaleuca, Ylang Ylang, Serenity Calming Blend, Elevation Joyful Blend, or Breathe Easy Air Respiratory Blend to help heal and balance this chakra.

You could say this positive affirmation to yourself to help keep this chakra balanced: "I am giving and receiving love effortlessly and unconditionally."

THROAT CHAKRA – VISHUDDHA

This throat chakra is also called vishuddha. Vishuddha simply means to purify. This is the first one of the three spiritual chakras. This chakra can enhance your communication skills. It lets you speak your mind without worrying about it. This chakra makes you assertive and audible when you speak. It can help you artistically. This chakra can help you express your emotions, specifically the ones that use self-responsibility.

This chakra oversees truth, words, and communication. It has the color blue and is located in the throat. It controls the larynx regions, tongue, mouth, neck, jaw, parathyroid, and thyroid. The element that corresponds to this chakra is space or ether, and hearing is the sense.

This chakra is important for emotional well-being and communication. If the chakra is aligned, you will be able to have very smooth communications. You can speak your truth without worry. You will also be able to make good presentations. True expression isn't something that will come easy. There is a fine line between saying what you mean and staying diplomatic. It is easy just to say what others might want to hear instead of telling the truth. You might have a fear of being accepted, or being judged by others could hinder your truthful expression. Take ten minutes and close your eyes. See the color going from your throat to your mouth. Watch as this blue fire heals your vocal cords.

If the chakra isn't aligned, you may have a fear of speaking, hoarseness, or sore throat. If the chakra isn't activated, you might experience depression and other negative emotions.

. . .

If this chakra is inactive, you might experience hypothyroidism, inaudible speaking, and an inability to express yourself. If the chakra is overactive, you might experience hyperthyroidism, loud talking, excessive talking, criticism, and gossip.

If you want to heal this chakra, you could use the yoga pose plow. You could also use crystals like sodalite, lapis lazuli, turquoise, angelite, apatite, celestite, aquamarine, blue lace agate, and apatite to help heal and balance this chakra. You could also use some essential oils like Birch, Lavender, or Oregano, to help heal and balance this chakra. You could say the following affirmation daily to help keep this chakra balanced: "I am speaking clearly and truthfully with grace and ease."

THIRD EYE CHAKRA – AJNA

The third eye chakra is also called Ajna. Ajna means to know. It is the center to access your higher self, telepathy, insight, inspiration, and farsightedness.

This chakra brings better spiritual understanding and self-awareness. If it is balanced, you will make very good decisions. You will have wisdom and understand all spiritual matters.

This chakra controls two emotional responses: insight and intuition. If this chakra is aligned, you will have more intuition. You will be able to see in people's minds and see into the future. This is the most famous chakra of the seven.

This chakra's color is indigo and is located in the middle of your forehead between the eyebrows. If it is in alignment, you will have visualization, dream recall, creativity, and intuition.

We experience the world through the five senses. Before you were born, you could hear noises such as your mother's heartbeat and voice and the muffled noises from outside. You experienced taste, touch, and could even see some light. Since the moment of your birth, you have associated experiences with what you perceive with your senses. You have trusted your senses to what you hear, see, touch, smell, and taste. Sense perception is wonderful in experiencing life, but it can limit you when you try to expand your awareness.

There was a time when you needed to count on your inner knowing and intuition. Before we had modern technology, we had to rely on cues from the world around us and our primal instincts to help guide us. Squirrels know when to gather food, and birds know when a hurricane is coming in, we humans have intuitive senses, too. We have just lost touch with it, along with our ability to trust it.

If this chakra is overactive, you will have a lack of focus, nightmares, and headaches. If it is underactive, you won't be able to visualize or imagine.

• • •

If you want to heal this chakra, you can use the crystals purple fluorite, amethyst, lapis lazuli, lepidolite, blue quartz, sodalite, or charoite. You could use essential oils like Immortelle Anti-Aging Blend, Clary Sage, Past Tense Tension Blend, Lemongrass, or Intune Focus Blend. You can say this positive affirmation daily to help keep this chakra in balance: "I am tuned into the Divine to follow the path towards my purpose."

CROWN CHAKRA – SAHASRARA

This chakra controls enlightenment and understanding. It either has the color of light purple or clears. It can be located at the top of the head. It has been called the thousand-petal lotus chakra. The lotus is a symbol of Buddhist and Hindu religions. It gets nurtured; it grows and emerges out of muddy water. It blooms in places of no brightness. Its beauty is unique to the environment that doesn't have any vibrancy and is monotonous.

When you can unfurl this seventh chakra, you will emerge through all the confines of your physical body, your ego, your mind, and your intellect. You will even be able to push beyond the soul that keeps you tied to Samsara, which is the looping cycle of birth and rebirth. You will be freed from desire. A white light will surround your body, and you will stand above your murky surroundings.

It controls thoughts, and you will have enlightenment, wisdom, universal connection, and spiritual awakening.

When you start trying to balance this chakra, you might be looking for a divine and higher connection.

With this chakra, you will be able to get rid of all negative things. It will feel like you don't even live in the world. This is why all the chakras have to be aligned, so the Muladhara will still ground you when you feel enlightened.

You will be able to understand why you are here, forgive others when they wrong you, and understand people better. With this chakra, the infinite and finite aspect of being human meets. This experience has been described as "an awakening," "ego depletion," and "enlightenment."

There are several responses that accompany this chakra when it is in balance. These are wisdom and peace. If it is overactive, you might feel superior to others and have frequent daydreaming.

If it is underactive, you might experience more skepticism. If it isn't active, you might have problems thinking. To heal this chakra, you can try doing the yoga poses wheel and headstand. You could also try healing it by using crystals like Clear Quartz, Amethyst, Diamond, Lepidolite, Sapphire, Moonstone, Sugilite. You could use essential oils like Frankincense, Helichrysum, Lemon, Roman Chamomile, Zendocrine Detox Blend, Melissa, DDR Prime Cellular Complex, and Sandalwood. You can say the positive affirmation of: "I am one with my higher self and one with the Divine."

DEVELOPING YOUR CHAKRAS

THE CHAKRAS and the world are closely connected. The world can affect the chakras, and the chakras can affect the world. They are supposed to work in harmony with one another. The power to balance the chakras lives within you and everybody and can be accomplished through crystals, energetic healing, nutrition, self-reflection, yoga, meditation, or by getting into a high vibration setting by looking into your emotions.

When you have balanced chakras, you feel the best. Most people who are familiar with chakras, and very well connected to them, can feel them and will recognize when a certain chakra is out of balance. Since the chakras work congruently in our lives and everything in the world is connected, our lives will move in patterns that correspond to the chakras.

We all have one chakra that remains dominant for a seven-year period. From birth until we turn seven, our root chakra is the dominant one. From ages eight to 14, the sacral chakra is the dominant one. During these seven-year cycles, we are also climbing the same seven chakras each year. That means, while the sacral chakra may be the overall dominant one from age eight to 14, that first year, the root chakra is more active, and we will experience a need for security and fear. The second year of the cycle will be marked by an active sacral chakra, and so on until you reach the crown chakra in the last year of the seven-year cycle. To help you understand, here is a year-by-year breakdown of how your chakras work at any given age.

One Year Old: The root chakra is associated with being grounded, family, and security. At this age, our instincts, thoughts, and actions are all tied to this chakra. In the first year of life, we enter this cycle associated with the root chakra. This is when we are experiencing everything for the first time. We are just getting used to our planet, and we fear everything, including our feelings.

Two Years Old: At age two, we remain in the cycle of the root chakra, but we are starting to focus on the Earth's elements. We start to develop feelings because we are now tied with the sacral chakra. This chakra is concerned about emotions, creativity, and sexuality. We develop strong attachments to the people we love, and we develop preferences such as dislikes and likes.

Three Years Old: While still in the root chakra cycle, we are now connected to the solar plexus. This chakra is our "I am" presence. It is where we connect with our sense of self. It is the way we start to understand how we are connected to the world. At this age, we begin to understand ourselves and how we relate to others. We begin to really look at the world.

Four Years Old: We are still in the root chakra but are entering the heart chakra. This chakra relates to connections and love with both others and ourselves. If it is out of balance, the heart can become overbearing and afraid of love. If it is balanced, it lets love shine through. We are still figuring out our connection to the world and getting more familiar with it as we start expressing love to friends and family. We begin becoming more social as we go to preschool.

Five Years Old: We remain in the root cycle but begin to enter the throat cycle. This chakra is about self-expression and communication. We also develop speaking and listening skills. We begin school and start speaking better and more.

Six Years Old: We remain in the root chakra but entering the third eye chakra. This chakra is about critically thinking, the pineal gland, and intuition. At this age, we start to think for ourselves more and can communicate things we know with others since we are beginning to understand them better.

Seven Years Old: We are entering into the last stage in the root cycle along with the crown chakra. This chakra connects us spiritually with the world. It ties our consciousness to a whole. We start to develop a curiosity for our world, especially the mysteries of the universe and the unknown.

By looking at this seven-year cycle year-by-year, you can really start to see this theme in all children. With ages one to seven, the root chakra rules them all, but a new chakra gets added with each passing year. Let's take a look at how other seven-year-cycles work. We won't continue with the year-by-year breakdown, but you'll continue to see the same pattern.

Ages 8 to 14: The sacral chakra rules this seven-year-cycle. This chakra is all about feeling and expressing emotions, creativity, and sexual energy. This is during a time when we will experience sexuality and will develop our first crush. Young ladies typically get their periods during this time, and both males and females will start to understand their sexuality. They also start to understand reproduction. During this time, most young people will have a relationship for the first time and will understand what both sexes represented.

Ages 15 to 21: During this time, the solar plexus chakra rules you. This shows us our sense of self, and we understand who we are as people and souls. Most young people will start experiencing angst and get more introspective or selfish as they figure out who they are. They begin to look objectively at who they are in relation to others and the way their personalities affect perspectives and relationships. People will have very strong dreams and hopes during this time in their lives. They understand what they want in life and what their purpose in this world is.

Ages 22 to 28: We begin to enter into the heart chakra. This is ruled by love for others and ourselves. Most people meet their significant others during this cycle because society puts pressure on young people to get married. Many people will develop a better love for themselves, which they will apply outwards into their relationships and appreciation for all people and life. Most people will begin to think about what they want to do to make their mark on the world because they have learned to appreciate the earth and everyone who lives on it.

Ages 29 to 35: This cycle represents the throat chakra. This chakra is in charge of communication skills and the ability to express yourself. Most people find their voice during this stage of life and have become comfortable with who they have become. This allows them to openly and freely express themselves. Most people will find their life's purpose or start to refine it since they developed a better ability to communicate exactly the things they want.

Ages 36 to 42: In this life cycle, we enter into the third eye chakra. This cycle is about synthesizing information, wisdom, and intuition. Many people will have epiphanies or understand the knowledge they have gotten from life until this moment in life. They know how to use this information efficiently. Most people will fall into their beliefs and let them govern their lives during this time if their third eye isn't in balance.

Ages 43 to 49: The last cycle relates to the crown chakra. This chakra relates to spiritual connections, collective consciousness, and spiritual awakenings. It is during this time that most people start to fear death. This usually means they have a blocked crown chakra. This cycle of life can cause a person's interest to peak in interconnectedness and spirituality. A lot of people develop a craving to understand the universe, and for knowledge, this often turns into a real-life "mid-life crisis."

The cycles will continue to repeat themselves throughout your lifetime in various ways.

CHAKRAS AND YOUR CONSCIOUSNESS

According to yogic tradition, the belief is that the chakras correlate to the universal soul where your soul can unite. They reflect the way in which the unified consciousness of humanity is divided to handle the various parts of earthly life. Every perception, every sense, every state of awareness, and every possible experience you could have, is all mapped out in your chakras. Instead of the specific, there are also elaborate mythological and pictorial associations that people have created. All of these myths and statements come from experiences and visions yogis have had as they awakened their chakras.

The body is known as "the Shrine of the Spirit," where the power of nature lives. Having a good understanding of the chakras suggests that knowledge of the yoga system will give you access to the ancient and rich reservoir of our natural wisdom.

The human experience is a demanding one and can damage our true nature. What things have you done in order to handle life and function? What things have you been neglecting? Have you felt that your uniqueness has been misplaced? Why have you allowed yourself to go so far out of balance? What have you lost sight of?

The regular and unstimulated energizing or awakening of your chakras will take a natural growth progression, which will happen over a seven-year period. This is only a basic progression, and your chakras are going to overlap and act with one another. We will always have their functioning throughout our life, but each will lead at various times, depending on where we are in life. Energetically, life's path seems to act like a spiral, where we view our life issues from various perceptive windows of our chakras. Through these portals, we interpret our relationships and personal history. The same questions and issues can come up at various times in our lives as we start to spiral upwards, but they also have different implications as the vantage points change.

Insights into the challenges that you have worked through and making sure that you live in a conscious partnership with your chakras will empower you to experience complete consciousness that is inside of you. All you need to learn is that you already possess the energy you need to live your highest destiny.

KEEPING YOUR CHAKRAS BALANCED

THE IDEA of balancing your chakras isn't a black and white concept. It actually involves various techniques and has several meanings. A simple definition, though, is a process in which the chakra's energy is brought to a harmonious and well-functioning state. Balancing your chakras is only a section of the whole picture. Each chakra has to be able to function as a whole. If you take the time to look at the way each chakra works, you can see that they have a force that connects, and they interact energetically. This means when it comes to balancing your chakras, it is important that you not only think about each chakra individually but their neighboring centers and the energy that flows through the entire system.

COMMONS SIGNS THAT YOUR CHAKRAS ARE OUT OF BALANCE

When you have out of balance chakras, they will let you know there is a problem. It is up to you to pay attention to these signs and work to correct them.

1. Weight Issues

The chakras that are affected will be the sacral chakra, solar plexus chakra, and the root chakra. Most people think weight issues are caused by lifestyle, dietary, or behavioral problems along with exercise, but one cause most people don't consider is not being grounded. When we aren't grounded, it causes issues for the root chakra. If the root chakra is balanced, we will feel connected to nature. It won't matter what we might be facing in life; it makes us feel secure as all our basic necessities are being met. Most of us gain weight to help us feel grounded. Food is used as the support, but it is only superficial support and not a lasting one.

We might use weight as a buffer between the world and us when our self-esteem feels off or feel intimidated or attacked. If this is the case, our solar plexus chakra might be unbalanced. The solar plexus chakra is our center of power. It helps with confidence, self-esteem, and control.

At times we have problems feeling pleasure and getting in touch with our emotions. Suppose we bottle up feelings about what is happening around and in us, and we don't process the emotions that might have shaped our feelings about survival and self-worth. In that case, we won't experience pleasure when we eat, and our sacral chakra is unbalanced.

. . .

*I*f you have a severe problem with low body weight, an intense fear of gaining any weight, and your perception about your weight is distorted, you have probably been diagnosed with anorexia. People who suffer from anorexia restrict how much food they eat drastically. Bulimia is when someone eats a huge amount of food, and then they either take laxatives, make themselves throw up, or exercise excessively. Both of these disorders will judge a person's appearance harshly because they think they have to be severely thin to be worthy. They try to control their self-image because they believe they have physical flaws. An unbalanced solar plexus causes both of these disorders.

1. Mental Health Concerns

Every mental health concern out there could be connected to a chakra imbalance. Each mental health concern is connected to a different chakra. Anxiety could affect all of the chakras. It depends on the form of anxiety the person has. Anxiety is a part of our lives. When we develop an intense, persistent, or excessive worry that permeates our entire life, it becomes debilitating. If you have excessive anxiety, it could transform into terror or fear in minutes, which could lead to a panic attack. It can also affect our quality of life.

*I*f it's your crown chakra that is out of balance, you may feel as though you aren't connected to God, Goddess, Universe, Source, or Divine. If the anxiety is coming from an unbalanced third eye, you could feel anxious about the unknown, and you are unable to trust your intuition. You could worry about sharing how you really feel, expressing yourself, and communicating with others if your throat chakra is unbalanced. If you are feeling intimidated and overwhelmed by everything, your solar plexus may be out of balance. If you have an unbalanced sacral chakra, you may experience guilt or shame. Past traumas could cause this. If you experience anxiety around surviving, such as money, shelter, or food, then the root chakra is not balanced.

Moving away from anxiety, let's look at depression. The crown and heart chakra are most commonly the cause of depression. Depression happens for many reasons. It might pass through temporarily at times. At other times, it could be a presence in our lives that never goes away. For people who suffer from depression, it could be debilitating. Depression might feel like constant hopelessness, emptiness, or sadness. You might not have any pleasure in your daily activities and feel like life isn't worth living. It might affect your sleep or appetite, causing you to sleep too much or not sleep at all. You might even have thought about suicide or death.

When you are depressed, you will have a deep-seated feeling of loneliness. If you feel connected to the world and the Universe, the crown chakra is balanced and open. If you feel angry toward the Universe about your life, this shows your energy is out of harmony. Having an unbalanced heart chakra might cause depression because we aren't connected to ourselves.

Lastly, an unbalanced heart, root, and solar plexus chakra could cause panic attacks. Panic attacks happen when we are stuck with disabling, acute, and sudden anxiety. Feelings of impending doom can accompany these, shortness of breath, shaking, trembling, sweating, increased heart rate, pounding heart, and palpitations. These attacks can happen if we aren't connected to our heart chakra and don't listen to what it is telling us. The root chakra gets involved when fear and panic set in since our fear for survival gets triggered. If our heart chakra feels disconnected and in a constant state of fear, the solar plexus feels as if we have been punched in the stomach since our confidence and self-esteem live here.

1. Cancer

First, let me warn you that this is not meant to diagnose or treat any ailment, especially something as bad as cancer. However, balancing and aligning your chakras could assist regular cancer treatments if you are experiencing cancer. Cancer is a horrible disease, and nobody brings it upon themselves. It's unfortunate that many people have to face and fight, affecting all of the chakras.

Cancer occurs if the cells start to create and divide at an uncontrollable rate abnormally. They infiltrate and destroy good body tissue. This can happen on several different levels, and symptoms can vary depending on where the cancer is located. Symptoms could include thick areas under the skin, palpable lumps, skin changes, weight changes, fatigue, and many others. Factors that can increase cancer risk can include the environment, health conditions, family history, habits, and age. The Mayo Clinic has stated that most cancers happen in those who have no known risk factors. There is a chance, though, that cancer could be the result of deep hurt and resentment that has not been processed, denied, or ignored. It can manifest in toxic emotions, grief, or hatred that eats away at us.

. . .

*F*or example, cancers of the esophagus, larynx, and thyroid could be due to an unbalanced throat chakra. Lung cancer could be affected by the heart and throat chakras. Brain tumors would be connected to the crown chakra. Breast cancer could be connected to an unbalanced heart chakra. An unbalanced solar plexus chakra could cause cancers of the pancreas, intestines, liver, and stomach.

*T*hat said, if you are out in the sun for extended periods of time without proper protection, you smoke, drink excessive amounts of alcohol, or otherwise expose yourself to carcinogens on a regular basis, cancer likely has very little to do with chakras and more to do with lifestyle.

1. Headaches

*T*he crown and third eye chakras play a big part in headaches. If you suffer from headaches that aren't caused by some physical issue, it could be indicating that one of these chakras are out of balance. If your headache is in the front and includes pressure behind the eyes or sinus pressure, then you likely have an unbalanced third eye.

This headache could indicate that you have been focusing on your intelligence and fear your spirituality. You are likely only able to reality, and you ignore your intuition. When these types of headaches occur, it is because you are ignoring your inner wisdom. If you often have "hints" about things but don't act on them, you are ignoring your third eye. You may also feel as though you need to pursue new opportunities, but you choose not to. When you oppose intuitive hints, it can create an imbalance within the third eye chakra.

*I*f your headaches are felt at the top of your head, it could mean an imbalance in the crown chakra. This could mean that you struggle to accept trusting your path or seeing the larger picture. You could also struggle with finding faith in yourself and the connection you have to the divine. You might also feel unsatisfied or alone.

1. Reproductive Issues

*T*he chakras that are affected by this will be the solar plexus, root, and sacral chakras. If a woman can't conceive a child after many attempts for over one year, this is called infertility. Many will experience infertility, fear, and frustration that the woman experience creates a lot of stress and possibly shame. The sacral chakra is the one that is affected because it is associated with the genitals and womb but because it is the seat of all emotions. Most people who struggle with infertility will experience some extreme emotions. It makes them wonder: "Am I making the right decision?" "Do I even want to be a parent?" "Do I have the right partner?" "I might not even be a good parent." "How is this going to change my life?"

*T*here could be physical causes like a high follicle-stimulating hormone, lack of menstruation, low sperm count, poor egg quality, and other issues that could be to blame. Most of the time, there is high stress on the people who are trying to conceive. Since infertility could trigger family issues, the root chakra is involved, too. For people who are trying to conceive, this happens if they are trying to have a family if they aren't getting any support from their significant others. They might also be worried about passing on undesirable traits to their children. Making a new life is a challenge to a person's self-esteem, it can make them feel powerless, and this becomes a solar plexus issue since this is our power center.

If you suffer from uterine cysts or fibroids, your sacral chakra could be to blame. The Mayo Clinic states that uterine fibroids are growths that are in the uterus that aren't cancerous. They often happen during childbearing years. A lot of women have uterine fibroids that occur sometime in their lives. Most of the time, they don't cause any symptoms, but at others, they can grow to large-sized and cause pain during menstruation, when having a bowel movement, or when you are digesting food. They could cause problems breathing.

Cysts are sacs filled with fluid that are located on the ovaries. If there is a growth inside the uterus, it might be a sign that the sacral chakra is not balanced. There is an actual block to the reproductive area; the energy is telling you that there is a blocked energy flow inside. You might be holding onto toxic, negative, and old thoughts, feelings, or emotions that are flowing energy into dead ends. This could include relationships or jobs that you have outgrown or conflict with your relationships, reproduction, abundance, or creativity.

1. Joint Pain

Much like cancer, the area in which you experience the pain will tell you which chakra could be to blame. If you have problems with your hips that aren't caused by any physical trauma, there is usually a sacral chakra problem. Our hips hold onto a lot of unexpressed emotions that haven't been dealt with and that we keep avoiding. Since the sacral chakra is the seat of our emotions, we could cause imbalance if we don't honor our feeling.

For leg pain, the chakras that are affected will be the solar plexus or root chakra. Leg pain is usually linked to an imbalance in the root chakra. Leg pain might symbolize resistance to moving forward in life. This could manifest in self-sabotaging behaviors that are based on fear like the fear of failure or fear that we might get what we want. If this is the case, the root chakra could be linked to the solar plexus chakra, and both are out of balance. It is mainly a root chakra problem because of fear about clothing, water, food, housing, or bills.

If you are having neck pain, the chakra that is affected here is the throat chakra. If any physical trauma hasn't caused the neck pain, it could be that your throat chakra is out of balance due to the way you are interacting with the world. If we don't express ourselves honestly and openly or try to hide specific parts of ourselves like insecurities or fears from others, it can create imbalances to the throat chakra. There are many reasons why you might hold yourself back, but the end result is always the same neck pain.

. . .

If you have problems with sciatica, the sacral and root chakras could be to blame. Sciatica is characterized as pain that travels from the lower back down through the hip, buttocks, and down the leg. Most of the time, the pain is only felt on one side. If this is not caused by trauma, your sciatica pain could be telling you that you need to balance your root chakra. This chakra deals with problems of survival and your basic self. If a primal problem comes up, such as a fear that your basic necessities are going to be taken away, this could cause your root chakra to get out of balance. Sciatica tends to symbolize your fear about the future and money. That means, if you experience sciatic pain, you may not feel safe.

For other back pain, we will have to break it down into the different areas of the back. Again, if you have experienced physical trauma, then that is most likely the cause of the pain. The pain you could be experiencing could range from a dull ache that makes your back tighten to sharp acute pain that hinders your range of motion.

For upper back pain, it could be the throat and heart chakra. If you experience heartbreak or don't speak the truth, have issues with loving others, or threaten to love yourself, the tension could manifest as pain or tension in the upper back. You could feel as though you are holding back love, unloved, or unsupported.

. . .

For middle back pain, it could be your heart and solar plexus chakras. Everybody will experience issues with love, holding onto pain from the past, or you could face a power struggle, either way, you may feel pain or tension in the middle part of your back. This can often occur if you feel guilt from things you have done in the past or if you are stuck in the past for whatever reason.

For low back pain, the sacral and root chakras could be to blame. If you face challenges to your creative expression, relationships, or abundance, you could experience pain and tension in the low back. Holding back these emotions, or simply not processing them, and having issues with survival or basics needs, could cause pain here.

1. Asthma and Allergies

The chakra that is affected is the heart chakra. If you experience narrow airways and are producing excess mucus, it could trigger shortness of breath, wheezing, and coughing. If you have allergies, your immune system will make antibodies that recognize a certain allergen is harmful, even if it isn't. Both of these conditions cause problems with one's life. Sometimes these conditions can be caused by a compromised immune system and might cause inflammation of your digestive system, sinuses, airway, or skin. It could also cause respiratory distress. Since these are in the heart chakra, these reactions might be linked to this chakra is out of balance, especially if you have problems with compassion, love, heartache, and grief.

BENEFITS OF HEALING YOUR CHAKRAS

When you have aligned and balanced chakras, you will experience positive effects within yourself and outside of yourself. You could also notice some effects at home, school, and work, along with other areas of your life. When you feel your best, you will be happy and have faith in your life and path. This will mean that you are more productive and believe in yourself.

Everybody's chakras will require healing from time to time. The main thing is that you will have to investigate your life and figure out if you have something lacking. When you have learned how to spot a blocked chakra, you will always be on the lookout for any chakra that may require some cleaning so that you can enjoy the best health. Let's take a look at ten benefits that you can enjoy when you heal your chakras.

1. Self-acceptance and self-confidence

Having healthy chakras will give you a sense of self-confidence, self-acceptance, and self-love. If you feel confident about yourself, you can express yourself easier, and communicating with others will be hard for you.

Self-acceptance comes from self-realization. This is achieved by having balanced and healthy chakras. If you can realize yourself, you can embrace your weaknesses and strengths, and you will stop being intimidated by your weaknesses. You can work on them and then turn them into an advantage.

1. Having access to your inner wisdom

*H*aving healthy and balanced chakras helps you connect to a higher place where you can see your inner self. Once you know yourself inside and out, your self-awareness levels rise to understand your weaknesses and strengths better.

One strength you could access is an inner wisdom that guides you in living an impactful and meaningful life.

1. Better connection with your spirit

*W*hen you can unblock your crown chakra, you will have a stronger connection to your Divine Source. Once you realize your Divine Source and can establish a great connection with them, you will be able to communicate and surrender all problems to your Divine Source, and this will give you peace.

*T*he chakra that is associated with your spiritual aspect is your crown chakra. If it is balanced well, it could bring you much spiritual enlightenment. You will find that balancing your yin and yang will be very easy.

1. Better expression

*I*f you have a blocked throat chakra, expressing yourself truthfully is hard. Just one blocked chakra can affect the flow of energy to the rest of the chakras, and this will affect your whole system. You will be able to express yourself easily if you have healthy chakras. This will result in better relationships, more joy in life, self-acceptance, and self-confidence.

1. Reduces anxiety and stress

When we have negative energy stored in our bodies, it could result in bad emotions like depression, anger, fear, anxiety, and stress. These all have negative tolls on our health. Healing your chakras might involve visualization and meditation. This helps you unwind and relax and reduces your chances of becoming depressed, anxious, or stressed.

1. Weight loss

Having unhealthy chakras can cause negative emotions like stress and low self-esteem. These negative emotions might lead to an unhealthy lifestyle that might result in obesity and weight gain in many cases.

When chakras are balanced and healthy, these emotions are kept away and reduce your chance of living an unhealthy life. When you unblock your chakras, you do yoga, which works your body, giving you some exercise. Various yoga poses can heal blocked chakras, letting energy flow throughout the body and getting rid of some weight.

1. Sleep better

When you have blocked chakras, you have stale energy in your body. This negative energy can lead to insomnia. The best way to heal blocked chakra is through meditation. This is the best way to deal with insomnia. Doing meditation the proper way can help you fall asleep easier, and you will sleep better overall.

1. Self-realization

Having healthy chakras will make you aware of who you are and help you understand your true purpose. Once you realize your reasons for living, you will be able to focus on things that matter and change your focus from things that don't add value to yours or other's lives. When you know who you are, you will be on course to having the very best in life.

1. Passion for life

When you can connect to the spiritual realm, you can see the true purpose and meaning of life. This will increase your enthusiasm for life since you have become a purpose-driven person. One who knows why they are alive has passions to achieve their goals when compared to people who don't know why they are alive. It makes you a person others want to be around and share their journey with.

1. Releasing bad energy in healthy ways

When you have unbalanced chakras, you have a lot of negative energy inside you. It doesn't have to be that way since healing your chakra could help you purge all your negative emotions. Negative energy can be manifested as bad emotions such as shame, guilt, fear, and anger. When you have the energy wheels spinning in balance, there can't be any negative or stale energy trapped in you. It gets purged to make room for all the positive energy.

While healing your chakras can make you feel better, it's not going to make life easier. You will still face struggles, hurts, and heartache, but you will be able to handle those things better. They will no longer break you. You will learn how to handle these upsets better.

MYTHS ABOUT CHAKRAS

IT IS VERY common for anything in life to be surrounded by misinformation and myths. These myths get created when people don't take the time to learn about something they don't understand. They assume things and share those assumptions with others, and after a while, people start believing them to be facts. Several myths circulate about chakras. It's important that you are aware of what is true and what is a myth when it comes to chakras. It can greatly affect how you work with them.

1. Chakras don't really exist.

There are a lot of people out there that claim chakras don't exist. They refuse to acknowledge their existence, but the issue with this belief is that many areas in the world have their own definitions of chakras and proof that they do indeed exist. The seven chakras symbolize the nerve or energy centers that are present inside every human body. Energy, or prana, flows through the body through nadis. These are three channels similar to electric cables that take energy from the electricity center and supply the entire body's energy. The three nadis are Ida, Pingala, and Sushumna.

1. Opening the chakras is easy to do.

There is quite a bit of information out there about how you can open your chakras. In fact, doing so can help heal emotional or physical problems, among other issues. The truth about awakening your chakras isn't as easy as books make it seem. Opening your chakras is going to require a shift and change in your consciousness. This is going to require regular meditation for years. You can't just open the chakras by doing yoga poses, and it isn't only an emotional process.

1. Keeping your chakras balanced is going to improve your health.

This is one of the biggest misconceptions out there. Yes, balancing your chakras can improve your health. Your chakras' health also depends on your psychological, physiological, emotional, mental, and physical condition. If you don't take the time to work on these problems directly, you won't heal your chakras. Then you will never see any improvement in your condition.

1. You have to make sure your chakras are perfect and balanced at all times.

*I*f anybody ever tells you that your chakras must be balanced and perfect at all times, then they are living in their own little world. In the real world, nothing can be perfect, and all things have their own little imperfections. The world is unpredictable and changes all the time, and this is how your chakras behave. They are always changing. They are responsive and flexible. They will adjust to physical and psychological factors that affect you daily. They will also change with your emotional and physical state. That is why they need to be normalized and balanced on a regular basis.

1. Professional healers can balance and open your chakra in a single session.

A lot of people like going to professional healers like Acupressurists and Reiki healers to heal and balance their chakras, and they do so thinking it will happen in a single session. This is a big problem. It will always take more than a single sitting and more help than a professional healer can give you to open and balance your chakras fully. It requires you to want to be healed in the first place.

*Y*ou have to take charge of your emotions and body in order to be healed. Going to a professional healer is great, but you can't expect them to do all of the work for you.

1. There are only seven chakras.

This is a controversial topic and not necessarily a myth. Most people believe that we only have seven chakras in the body, and that isn't completely wrong. But, Yogic text does mention that there are many chakra systems that move throughout the body. Some believe that we have as many as 12 chakras, and others think there are many more work systems. The seven chakras that we are all familiar with, though, is where beginners need to start and are enough to work with for the most part.

1. Chakras are only "things" that live within the body.

Everybody needs to understand that chakras aren't material things. There are people who may not have thought about what this means. We speak as though an autopsy is going to reveal a string of different colored lotuses traveling through the center of our body. That's not what is going to happen. Chakras are energy channels on a plane of consciousness that results in psychosomatic functions and experiences. They are focal points for spirituality and meditation. They are abstract structures and not something physical.

1. The main purpose of working with chakras is to treat illnesses.

If you read the ancient Vedic text, chakras mean wheels and are the seven centers in the body that, if opened, can unfold to unforeseen realms. This has been the main goal of many people, especially those who want to become one with the Universe.

. . .

Most people today want to balance and open their chakras simply to treat emotional pain and physical illnesses. They don't deal with the consciousness and awareness of their Supreme Self. This is what has happened to yoga. Yoga has become nothing more than gymnastics, where doing a few asanas means you have become a yogi. The goal of yoga is to meet the Divine Source or our Supreme Consciousness by attaining the Samadhi through meditating. This, sadly, has been forgotten.

1. You are unable to control chakras.

Many people think you don't have any power over your chakras, and you can't balance them by yourself. The truth is the old saying: "Where there is a will, there is a way," holds true with controlling your chakras. The solar plexus chakra can help strengthen your inner desire, fire, and will. It doesn't matter what problems you are dealing with; you can harness this power and reach any goal you want to accomplish. This is true for every chakra in your body. They give you energy for many different tasks.

1. You only need to worry about the top chakras.

Most people want to only focus on the top chakras, like the throat, third eye, and crown chakra. These chakras focus on inner and spiritual growth, and people often forget that they have to balance from the bottom chakra to the top so that they work together.

The heart chakra is responsible for balancing out the bottom and top chakras. Before you try to focus on your third eye and crown chakra, you have to make sure that you have worked on your lower ones.

The root chakra is your physical life—the sacral deals with the emotions. The solar plexus is your power. If you ever plan on becoming successful in life, you have to make sure those chakras are balanced, as well as your remaining four chakras. That's why everything you read about will take you from the root chakra up to the crown. Once you have dealt with physical and emotional problems, you are ready to turn to your purpose in life. That's how you are supposed to balance your chakras.

1. Healers can get rid of all of your problems and Karmic baggage.

There is a law of cause and effect that is active in this Universe, and it is responsible for everything that goes on in the world. If you think that all of our actions from this and previous lifetimes, or your Karma, can be done away with by someone in just a few sessions is so completely wrong. The intensity of your Karma can be reduced, and you can increase your willpower when you balance your Karma, but no one in healing sessions can remove all the baggage. We have to think about these points before we move toward the path of balancing our chakras.

1. The chakras are simply energy sources.

*V*isualize a whirlpool. This whirlpool isn't water, but a vortex of water. This same principle applies to chakras. They aren't sources of energy; they are places where energy moves and gathers. Chakras are balls of spinning energy that is three dimensional that absorb and emit energy from the world. To balance and heal our chakras, we have to call outside sources such as pure Spirit energy, grounding earth energy, or channel Reiki energy.

1. How are you really supposed to pronounce the word chakra?

*D*o you remember learning this tongue twister when you were young? "How much wood could a woodchuck chuck if a woodchuck could chuck wood?" Now repeat, "chuck, chuck, chuck," now add "ra," and you got it: "chuck-ra." In the official translation convention for Sanskrit, the "c" gets pronounced as "ch" in "church." You might see "cakra" and "chakra." It doesn't matter how one spells; it just remembers woodchuck.

1. The sacral chakra only controls sex.

*T*here are a lot of desires that can play out through karma and instinct. We have a natural desire to gain freedom and experience, express ourselves, and to live. Instead of thinking about certain desires as exclusive to certain chakras, you need to think about desire as a natural state as humans and the foundation of life. Remember that every school of yoga supports mastery, transmutation, or transcendence of sensual desires even though they might differ in how the transcendence occurs.

IMPROVING YOUR CHAKRA HEALING PROCESS

EVERYBODY NEEDS to have clear energy flowing through us. Without that healthy energy flowing through the chakras, you will end up feeling depressed and empty, just like somebody pulled the plug on everything you have ever wanted. If there is a blockage in your energy centers, it will become a power outage that makes you feel horrible, but you can take steps to clear them. The power never leaves you; all you have to do is get it flowing again.

You embody a complex system from your root chakra at your tailbone all the way up to your crown chakra on top of your head. This system receives energy from the world around you and sends energy back out to the world in a healthy cycle. When your energy centers are balanced and clear of any blockages, these centers are spinning little wheels that keep you healthy. With time, emotional upsets, life, and trauma, it can impair this free flow of your chakras.

In a couple of chapters, you will be learning several ways to help heal your chakras. But, to help make sure those techniques work to the best of their abilities, the following seven steps can help supercharge your energy clearing exercises. They are all super easy, and anyone can do them.

Return to the Earth to Help Your Root Chakra

Go outside and spend some time with nature. Take a long walk in the park, or go for a hike. If you can take your shoes off and walk barefoot for a while, it will create a new foundation for you. It will help you to ground in the world around you and connect back with the Earth. It will leave you feeling present and have a sense of safety, and it will help to strengthen up your root chakra.

Get Into Healing Water to Help Your Sacral Chakra

If you can get to a beach and immerse yourself in the ocean, that is the best thing to do. If not, then fill your bathtub with some warm water, sea salt, and baking soda. This will help to strengthen your sacral chakra. Your sexual chakra controls all of your pleasures and can easily become marred by feelings of shame and guilt. While you are in the water, picture all of these feelings of shame and guilt dissolving away as the waterworks to restore the purity of your true self.

Move to Help Your Solar Plexus Chakra

Your solar plexus chakra loves it when you move your body. It especially loves when you can get outside in the sunshine of a just risen sun or right as the sunsets. Any type of physical activity can help you to awaken and clear out your third chakra to bring you more willpower, self-esteem, and personal power.

Share and Accept Love to Help Your Heart Chakra

Your heart chakra holds the key to your compassion and loves it when you get to experience unconditional love. This love can be the love you have for yourself, others, everybody, and the world. If you have a pet, spend some time with it. Show it love, and they will return that love unconditionally. This is the best way to make sure you get a huge dose of compassion in your life. Finding ways to experience compassion and love is not that hard, even if you don't have a pet. You can spend some time at your local animal shelter. Those animals need all the love they can get.

Express Yourself to Help Your Throat Chakra

Your throat chakra doesn't like it when you don't allow yourself to express your truth. The fifth chakra allows you to speak up and be the real you. If you don't want to say something, you can write it down in a journal and be completely honest in your journal. Nobody else is going to read it, so say what you feel like you need to. Not only will it release some stress, but it will stimulate your throat chakra. When you have some free time alone or not alone, if your friends don't mind, crank up some music and sing your heart out. This will help to free up your fifth chakra, too. When you are talking with a person, communicate openly.

Listen to the Inner Your to Help Your Third Eye

Your third eye is where your higher self lives and provides you with clarity. Having a daily meditation practice is an essential part of healing your energy and chakras. It will also awaken your sixth chakra and allow you to turn into the wisdom you already have inside you. You will find that you start to trust your intuition more. Meditation will help you get rid of that mental chatter that you have to live with daily, which will allow you to see things more clearly.

Connection with the Spirit to Help Your Crown Chakra

Your crown chakra is what allows you to connect with the universe and your higher powers. It is what controls your consciousness. Like the third eye chakra, meditation is the perfect way to connect with the higher powers and to boost the seventh chakra. Another way to clear out your crown chakra is through prayer. This prayer can be anything that you want it to be. You can pray to the Universe, God, whomever you believe in. It can also be a simple mantra that you chant each day. Taking some time to connect with nature can also help with clearing out and charging your crown chakra, or really, any of your chakras. Talk to your higher power every day and ask them for some guidance and picture peaceful and positive outcomes for whatever is going on in your life or in the world.

As you work on balancing and clearing your chakras, you will notice that you feel better and have a new energy that can easily flow through you. Your chakra system will take in and release energy like it is meant to. With everything working together, you will feel happier and healthier.

COMMON RISKS TO OPENING CHAKRAS

WE'VE LOOKED at information on your chakras and what they do for your body. We've also looked at the signs of blocked chakras and the benefits of opening them. Before you start working on your chakras, you also need to understand the dangers of opening them too quickly.

There are lots of great reasons to focus your energy on your chakras and make sure that they are open and working. When you have a balanced heart chakra, it will help you with all of your relationships. When your throat chakra is open, you are able to share your truth. It's also a good thing to make your chakras a priority, but if you move too fast, it can end up having bad consequences.

When your chakras are open, more energy will come into you. Blocked chakras will create stagnant energy, and it won't freely pass through you. Blockages should be removed, but you need to go at it gradually. Going too fast will bring in a lot of energy.

What happens when you open your chakras too quickly will depend on which chakra it is and how much energy you are using. To figure this out, think about what the chakra does for you.

The heart chakra, as you know, controls your ability to love. A blocked heart chakra could cause you to avoid relationships. When your heart chakra is opened too quickly, a rush of energy could overwhelm you and kick your heart chakra into overdrive. This could cause you to become needy in your relationships. You could also end up connecting with people too quickly. This makes the chakra no better than it was when it was blocked.

When you have a blocked third eye chakra, you aren't in touch with your intuition. You likely focus on logic, and you don't follow your gut. If you open this one too fast, it will send a rush of energy that will overwhelm you and the chakra. You could end up experiencing intuitions that can scare you. You may end up with psychic abilities that you aren't able to control. Spirits from other realms could end up talking to you, and you don't know how to control it. Again, this makes your chakra no better than it was when it was blocked.

While this may seem scary, it doesn't mean you should avoid opening them all together. Instead, all you need to do is make sure that you open them slowly. You want to be the tortoise and not the hare when it comes to opening your chakras.

You should stay away from anything or anyone that promises to help you open your chakras quickly. You need to be patient. You have to trust that your chakras will open in time without you going to extremes to get them to open.

There are some different side effects that you can experience when you are opening your chakras. Most will only happen if you allow them to open too quickly.

Over Stimulation of Your Senses

This will often happen with an overactive root chakra. When the root chakra is opened, you become more aware of the earth, the way it feels, sounds, looks, and smells, among other things. When you open that chakra too quickly, you will be overloaded with these sensations. You could even find it hard to function because the sun is too bright, or you smell the flowery perfume of the lady sitting five seats behind you on the bus. It can drive you crazy with everything that you will start sensing.

. . .

Detachment

This happens when your crown chakra is opened. When you take the spiritual journey to work with your chakras or any spiritual journey is normally done somewhat alone. We each have to walk our own journey. A lot of people will start noticing that they gravitate towards secluded moments, especially when the crown chakra opens too quickly. This may end up causing you to feel disconnected.

Déjà vu

This could happen with the crown chakra and your third eye chakra. While this is often a sign of having successfully opened a chakra, it can happen in excess, which means you opened them too quickly. This can become overwhelming and can also spill over into your dreams, causing vivid or frightening dreams.

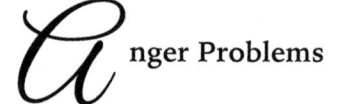

Anger Problems

When you have an overactive solar plexus chakra, you could experience more anger than usual. This could mean that you just feel angry for no reason, or your fly off the handle at the drop of a hat. This could also involve a new sense of perfectionism and being too critical of yourself and others.

Sleep Disturbances

A lot of people find that they don't sleep as much once they have healed their chakras. This also means that if you open them too quickly, it can cause unrest at night. You might find that you can't get comfortable when you're sleeping. All of this means that you could end up feeling irritable and unstable.

Unusual Bladder Activity and Reproductive Problems

This tends to happen with an overactive sacral chakra. This can cause aches and pains in your lower abdomen, as well as unusual bladder habits and urinary problems. For women, it could also mess with their menstrual cycle. It can also create more serious problems like endometriosis, testicular or prostate problems, ovarian cysts, and infertility if not taken care of.

Neglecting Emotional Care

. . .

You can become too absorbed in caring for others if you allow your chakras to open too quickly. This will cause you to neglect yourself, which will end up causing more problems.

Meditation is the perfect way to heal your chakras, but you need to do it in a slow way so that you don't become overwhelmed. Prayer is also another way to create the intention to heal your chakras. Wearing crystals that help you to balance your chakras is a great thing to do. These crystals will slowly raise your vibration and change the energy that surrounds your chakras. Color working is another great way to balance out your chakras.

Healing anything is a slow process, and this is true for healing your chakras. You need to let things happen by themselves, and you will begin to see a difference that won't end up leaving you overwhelmed.

MISTAKES MADE WHEN OPENING CHAKRAS

Healing your chakras and energy will provide you with amazing results in your life if you are able to use them correctly. Like most things in life, people will often make mistakes when it comes to opening their chakras. The more you try to avoid these mistakes, the easier your journey is going to be.

With the spiritual awakening that the planet is experiencing, more people have started to turn to energy healing exercises. Often though, things won't go the way you planned, or something will seem to be interfering. Energy healing is supposed to make noticeable changes in your life. This can range from your actual emotions to your belief systems.

Most of the time, the changes that happen through this form of healing are typically referred to as miraculous, but this only happens if things go correctly. If your healing winds up not being miraculous, then you may be making one of these mistakes.

1. Stopping When You Start to Feel Better

Energy or chakra healing works kind of like antibiotics; you have to keep going even after you start feeling better. You have to continue healing when you feel good and when you feel bad. Otherwise, you're not getting the full experience.

To really get into your issues and reach the layers that will make the best changes, you have to be able to deal with things when you are feeling better. This means that your system will be able to handle more work.

Working on your chakras regularly, especially when you are in a good space, will allow you to get ahead of those bad moments and possibly avoid them altogether. This will allow you to have a smoother life, which is what you are hoping to achieve in the first place.

1. Not Maintaining

Your chakras are just like any other system, they require regular maintenance, or it's going to end up becoming clogged up again. If you only work on things when you are in some sort of crisis, your body is going only to neglect everything else. When you have regular sessions, you will be able to keep your chakras clear and in line with each other so that you don't experience a back up of energy.

1. Trying to Just Heal Physical Problems

Chakra healing helps you spiritually, mentally, physically, and emotionally. But, a lot of people tend to heal their chakras just to get rid of physical problems. This is only a part of what chakra healing can do, so there is no sense in pigeonholing yourself in just trying to fix physical problems. Expand your reasons for every part of your life.

1. Not Allowing Enough Time

After you have been working with your chakras for a while, you see a few immediate results in several different areas. However, when you start out, you should expect about three weeks for things to start to shift and change. This means that people won't see results as quickly as they had hoped. This will cause them to want to stop because they don't think it's working.

To help remedy this problem, keep a log every day to write out what you are feeling.

1. Waiting Until Issues Have Passed

This may happen right when you start to heal your chakras, or it could happen a few weeks later, but you will find yourself feeling sick or experiencing a lot of stuff. Don't let this keep you from continuing with your healing. These are the days when you need it the most. Healing sessions can help you to push through these issues and bring you to new energy levels.

. . .

Most of the time, the issues, whether you are sick or have a lot of crap going on due to your energy shifting. The negative energy has to be shifted somewhere so that it can be released. Work through these moments while continuing to heal, and you'll be amazed at how good you feel.

1. Constantly Thinking About It

Humans love to complain about things. It's also really easy for us to get caught up on thought and pick at it, breaking it down and dissecting it over and over again. When you have done some healing work, you will likely go through a 24 to 72 hour period where your old energy will move out of your body. This can manifest in several different ways.

If you constantly think about something you are worried about, it will only reinforce that problem and those pathways, and it will trap that in your system. This won't allow it to be released from your system after a healing session.

1. Not Believing

When you hear or experience the power of chakra healing, it is quite easy to fall into stunned belief and feel as if it couldn't possibly be true. Since your head is what makes your world, it will create your world in everything.

When you don't believe that chakra healing works, then it's not going to work for you. Energy healing works with your belief system. That's why you need to make sure that your belief system and your healing work align. When you constantly tell yourself that you don't believe it will work, you will only unravel your work.

*I*f you can get these common mistakes under control, you will see the benefits of chakra healing.

TECHNIQUES TO HEAL CHAKRAS

As you have come to understand throughout this book, chakras can become blocked due to trauma, repressed memories, guilt, and denial, among other problems. These, often psychological, issues will prevent your energy from flowing freely through your body. When chakras are blocked, you can experience any number of negative ailments. The good news is, it won't take all that long to get your chakras back into balance. Before we get into specific healing techniques, like reiki and mantras, here are few miscellaneous techniques that you can try that don't require special skills or equipment.

1. Visualization

To perform a visualization, find a quiet and comfortable place to sit and close your eyes. Start by visualizing all of your chakras. As you do this, begin with your root chakra and slowly work your way up to the crown chakra. Spend a few minutes with each of your chakras and visualize them with their correlating color: red for root, orange for sacral, yellow for solar plexus, green for heart, blue for throat, indigo for the third eye, and purple for the crown. This visualization will give you the chance to connect with each of your chakras, and it is a great way to help fix a blocked one.

1. Deep Breathing

You can use this along with the visualization process we just discussed. As you fill your lungs up with air and slowly release the breath, the gradual movement of your belly and the visualization of your chakras will allow you to make a connection with each one. This will work the best when you have some time to sit quietly, free from disturbances and distractions.

1. Sound

The body is made up of main water, and since the chakras live within the body, and vibrations will stir up all of the water, the vibrations can be used to connect with your chakras. There are a few chakras, like the throat and heart, that can be unblocked using music. So, turn on your radio, play your favorite CD, or turn on your favorite Spotify playlist, and sing your heart out. Listening to soothing music can also help to calm your mind.

1. Jewelry

You can easily wear several pieces of jewelry to heal your chakras. The first thing you have to do with the jewelry is to set an intention for the piece. To make this work a little better, start with only one piece of jewelry. Wear that piece for a few days, and keep your focus on the intention of healing one of your chakras. Once you can feel a change, add a second piece of jewelry and set the intention to heal a different chakra. Keep doing this until you have a piece of jewelry associated with each of your chakras.

When you are wearing these pieces, you will notice that you feel at peace. The healing of your chakras will happen on a subconscious level, so you don't have to stay focused on it all of the time.

1. Flower Essences

These are a lot like aromatherapy, but they are little bottles of liquid that can help you heal your chakras. They are vibrational remedies that you can mix into water or drop some under your tongue, and they will bring you powerful positive energy changes. While this may sound like aromatherapy oils, they are very different. They don't have a smell. Instead, it is the plants' vibrational essence that has been preserved in a mixture of water and brandy. These can be found in most health food stores, or you can find them online. These are some specific flower essences for each chakra:

- Pine – root

- Crabapple – sacral
- Mustard – solar plexus
- Holly – heart
- Honeysuckle – throat
- Star of Bethlehem – the third eye
- Wild rose – crown

1. Aromatherapy

*A*romatherapy is a great tool when it comes to relaxing and re-centering. Most massage therapists will use aromatherapy to help relax their clients during a massage. That's because they are a great way to relax. It is also an amazing way to heal your chakras, especially when you use the scents that correspond to your chakras. This is perfect to use during your meditations to help up the power of your healing.

- Root – vetiver and patchouli
- Sacral – jasmine and ylang-ylang
- Solar plexus – lemon, tangerine, and orange
- Heart – rose and geranium
- Throat – clary sage, sage, and rosemary
- Third eye – peppermint and rosewood
- Crown – lavender, cedar, and frankincense

1. Stones and Crystals

*E*very chakra has a stone and crystal associated with it. The easiest thing to do is to find stones that match the color of each of the chakras. You will then activate and energize the stones for the purpose of healing your chakras. The vibration and the color of the crystals will do all of the healing work. There are some stones that you can use that will heal several chakras. The following are some crystals and the chakra that they can help heal.

- Root – hematite, smoky quartz, agate, garnet, ruby, and bloodstone
- Sacral – carnelian and moonstone
- Solar plexus – citrine, amber, and tiger's eye
- Heart – rose quartz, green jade, and emeralds
- Throat – aquamarine and turquoise
- Third eye – sodalite and lapis lazuli
- Crown – alexandrite and amethyst

KUNDALINI YOGA

Kundalini is an important life force that lies coiled up at the base of your spine. This energy is one of the strongest forces that can awaken all of your chakras and bring you to full enlightenment. Many people like to use a visualization of a serpent being awakened and rising up, which is exactly what your kundalini energy will do if it is awakened properly.

*Y*oga is a form of exercise that uses a combination of breathing exercises, stretches, and meditations to help improve your body's function, which will allow your energy to circulate. This form of exercise will bring about a better connection between your body, mind, and soul.

Kundalini yoga is a yoga that has been designed to help awaken your kundalini energy. It is made up of several breathing exercises and stretches that will help to clear out your chakras so that your energy can flow freely.

It is best to make sure that you are in a well-ventilated room that is quiet when you practice any of these kundalini yoga practices. Make sure that you have a comfy yoga mat to practice on.

Yoga Practice #1

1. Start out by setting an intention for your yoga practice.

This intention can be anything that you want, such as clarity, understanding, calm, or openness. You can use a few mantras to help you set your intention, such as:

"I am thankful for the inner strength I have, and I release my energy to heal."

. . .

"I embrace my power."

"I ask my body to free my life force."

You can come up with your own intentions and mantras depending on your mood at the moment, but you want to make sure that it will help you to create a goal for your practice.

While sitting on your yoga mat, breathe regularly for a couple of minutes. Focus your intention on your breath, noticing how it feels as it moves in and out of your nose. Allow positive energy to run through your body. As you breathe out, release any of your negative emotions that have been trapped in your body. Sit like this for a few minutes until you have begun to feel calm.

Put your feet flat on the mat a move into Crow Pose. To get into a crow, bring yourself in a low squat. Your feet should be flat on the mat, and your bottom should be a few inches off the ground, and your knees together. Bring your arms out in front of you so that they are in line with your shoulders. After a few moments, come to a standing position. Remain standing for a few seconds and then return to the deep squat you were in earlier, making sure your knees stay together.

. . .

*E*xtend your arms in front and keep them in line with your chest. As you remain in the squat, stay present, and breathe. Listen to how your body feels and let the energy flow through yours. This pose helps your root chakra. This will help you ground into the physical world. After being in this pose for a while, you will start to feel secure and safe, and you will believe in your ability for prosperity.

1. Move into a frog pose.

*I*n your squat position, shift your legs so that your legs open into a v-shape. Place your hands between your legs. You should look like a frog. Allow your eyes to close and breathe through your nose for a few seconds.

*S*traighten your legs with your hands remaining on the floor. Your head should be angled towards the floor and almost face-to-face with your ankles. Release your breath through your mouth, and hold the pose for a few seconds. Repeat this motion ten times and make sure that you keep your breath consistent; breathe in a while in the squat position and breathe out when you straighten your legs.

*T*his works your sacral chakra. This opens you up to creativity and sexual health.

1. Move into the stretch pose.

After your last repetition of the frog pose, ease down on your mat and lay flat on your back. Take a moment to breathe in and out through your nose. Your arms should be by your side and your legs straight out with your feet touching. Remain still for a couple of seconds and then carefully raise your feet and head five inches off the floor. Lift your arms up with your palms facing each other, and hold them so that they are level with your feet. Point your toes and keep your focus on them. Release the pose and then repeat eight to ten times.

While you are doing this, you want to use Breath of Fire. This is a series of quick short breaths. You should almost sound like a panting dog. You use only the nose to breathe. Your inhale is passive, and then push your exhale out hard.

This will bring you calmness by allowing more oxygen to run through your body. It also improves your blood circulation for your organs, which helps them to function properly. This will remove toxins, and strengthens your belly, and opens your solar plexus chakra. You will start to feel more power and confidence.

1. Move into the camel pose.

Shift yourself around so that you are on your knees. Flatten your lower leg on your mat with the tops of your feet on the floor and the soles facing up. Place your hands on your hips and then slowly bend back. When your hips feel open and feel that you can, reach your hands down and grab hold of your ankles. Allow your head to drop back. Close your eyes.

You need to use caution with this pose. If you aren't warmed up enough, and you force yourself back into the pose, you could end up hurting yourself. If you can't reach your ankles the first time, that's fine. Bend back as far as you feel safe doing. With more practice, you will be able to reach your toes. Do this slowly.

This pose will open up your heart chakra. You will start to experience compassion, love, and acceptance.

1. Move into cobra pose.

Slowly raise yourself up out of the camel pose and lower yourself down onto your belly and chest. Settle your hands on the mat under your shoulders, slowly push yourself up, lift your chest off the mat, and point your heart and head to the sky. Keep your feet, hips, and legs on the mat.

Make sure that you breathe while holding this pose, inhale through your nose, exhale through your mouth. Hold this for five sections and then lower back to your mat. Wait a few seconds, and repeat. Do this eight to ten times.

. . .

This will help to open up your throat chakra. You will find yourself being able to express yourself more freely, and you won't experience as much shyness.

1. Next, we will move into Guru Pranam.

This is called a child's pose. Once you have finished your last cobra repetition, move up so that you are sitting on your heels, and then bend forward so that your forehead is on your mat. Stretch your arms out in front of you, and let yourself relax onto your upper thighs. You can also keep your knees out, creating a v-shape, and allow your chest to rest between your legs.

This helps your third eye chakra. This will allow you to gain more intuition and help you transcend beyond your world. Make sure that you stay tuned to your body. Be mindful of your breath and allow your thoughts to flow. This will place you into a meditative state.

1. Move into the last pose, Sat Kriya.

This is your last pose in this kundalini yoga meditation practice. This pose is powerful and allows your life force to travel up through all of your chakras. This will send your energy through your bloodstream to your bones and organs.

. . .

Raise back up so that you are sitting on your heels. Stretch your back and neck up straight as you breathe. As you inhale, breath in positive energy, and as you exhale, breathe out negative energy. Release everything that isn't serving your body. When you exhale, bring your arms straight above your head and interlock your fingers. Extend your first fingers up to the sky.

As you sit in this position, chant "Sat Nam." Make sure that you say "Sat" as you breathe in and "Nam" as you breathe out. Sit in this position and do this for five to 20 minutes, or however long you feel you can hold this pose.

"Sat Nam" means "true vibration." This will help you to honor your truth and intuition. You already know what you need, no matter what happens to you.

This entire yoga practice can take only ten minutes or take as long as an hour. How long it will take will depend on you.

Yoga Practice #2

1. Get ready.

Get into a comfortable cross-legged position. Allow your breathing to slow down. Notice how it flows deep into your stomach and ribs, expanding them. Once you are

DEB LILITH

relaxed, put your hands in prayer and chant, "Ong Namo Guru Dev Namo," three times.

1. Move into leg lifts.

Slowly bring yourself to lie flat on your back with your arms against your sides. Breathe in through your mouth as you bring your legs up straight. Breathe out through your nose as you bring your legs down. The knees should stay straight. If you need to, you can put a blanket under your hips and one below your calves. Keep your motions smooth as you raise and lower your legs, following your breath. Do this for one to three minutes.

1. Move into rock pose.

As soon as you finish your leg lifts, go directly into rock pose. This is where you sit on your heels and keep your upper body straight. Place your hand on your shoulders. Breathe in through the mouth and raise your hips until you are on your knees in a kneeling position. As you move to your knees, allow your elbows to point back and your hips to point forwards. Your head should remain level. Breathe out through your nose and return to rock pose. Repeat this motion, following your breath, for one to three minutes. As you become warm, quicken your pace.

1. Move into a grind.

Come out of rock pose and return to a cross-legged position. Rest your hands on your knees and start to make large circles with your lower torso by rotating your bellybutton to the front, the right, the back, the side, and the front again. Let the rest of your body move naturally with these motions. It would help if you breathed in when your torso moves forward and breathe out when it moves back. Do this for one to three minutes. Halfway through, reverse your direction.

1. Move into a mudra.

Move from the cross-legged back into rock pose. Grasp your hands behind your back in Venus lock. For the Venus lock, interlace your fingers and place one thumb on the Mound of Venus of the other hand. This is the squishy flesh below the thumb. Normally, women will put their left thumb on the Mound of Venus on the right, and men will do the opposite.

This is a common mudra for kundalini yoga and is very balancing. This can be done at any point in your day if you are feeling unfocused or anxious.

Breathe in through your mouth and bring your forehead to the floor and lift your interlocked hands as far up as you can. Breathe out through your nose and raise back up. Repeat this breathing and movement for one to three minutes.

1. Relaxation.

Bring yourself down flat on your back and focus on your bellybutton and direct your flow of energy to it. This is where your awakening occurs. As you focus here, allow yourself to relax and keep your palms facing up beside your body. Picture your body melting into Earth. Notice as the universal light washes through you. Scan across your body so that every muscle relaxes. Stay here for five to seven minutes.

Yoga Practice #3

1. Become grounded with the Earth.

When you start this yoga session, you want to start out grounded. This will activate the root chakra and help you to feel more connected and safe. Mountain pose is the best way to make sure that you ground yourself in the Earth, and it's probably the easiest yoga position.

Stand on your mat with feet slightly apart. Make sure that your feet are firmly pressed into the mat and that you have your tailbone tucked under. Activate your stomach muscles, and allow your shoulders to relax. Make sure that the top of your head is pointed towards the sky. Bring the palms of your hands together so that they meet at your heart center. Take a deep breath in and feel how your feet are connected down through the Earth and how the top of your head reaches the sky. Notice the energetic connection that you have with the Earth and the sky. Picture a bright red light emanating from underneath your tailbone.

1. Move into a revolved triangle.

We're moving on up your chakras. You are now grounded and connected to Earth; you can now work on opening your emotions and pleasure. This is done through the revolved triangle pose. It helps to stimulate the lower abdomen and organs in this area. This will also make sure that you remain grounded.

From mountain pose, turn and step up to the top of your mat and step your left foot back. Keep your right toes pointed forwards and move your left foot so that it is parallel with the end of your mat. Keep your hips facing forward so that they are square with the front of your mat. Sit a yoga block to the inside of your right foot so that it is located under your face and rest your left hand on top of the block.

Gently rest your right hand in the crease of your hip and ease your hip back to keep it in line with the left hip. As you work to adjust the hips, slowly twist your upper body to the right. You can stay here if you wish, or you can start to extend your right arm so that it points to the sky, and the right shoulder is stacked over the left.

With each exhale and inhale, allow your spine to stretch more. Keep your mind on the region of your reproductive organs and picture an orange light glowing here. If you want to add some more intensity here, you can get rid of the block, placing your left hand on the mat and shifting your gaze up to your extended right hand. Remain here for a few more breaths and then return to pyramid pose.

. . .

Shift your feet so that the left foot is in front and the right in back, and repeat on the opposite side.

1. Move into boat pose.

Moving up to your solar plexus, you are getting ready to engage with your willpower and the internal heat that you have in your belly. The boat pose is the perfect way to engage your solar plexus chakra.

After coming out of the triangle pose on your left side, you slowly come to a seated position on your mat. Bend your knees so that your feet are flat. Put your hands next to your hips and raise your chest so that your spine is lengthened. Start to lean back until you feel your core engage slowly, but make sure that your heart stays lifted.

If this seems too easy, extend your arms in front of you and lift your lower legs so that they become parallel to your mat. As you maintain the pose, picture a yellow light circling around your chakra, building a fire in your belly. Keep holding boat pose for 15 to 30 seconds. Release your feet back to the mat and relax your belly for a few seconds, and then return to boat pose. Do this three to five times.

1. Move into a low lunge

Moving on up, we are now going to awaken our compassion and connection with other people. When you move into a low lunge, you will open up your heart space, and that should be your focus on this move.

Once you release your last boat pose, move to your hands and knees, and then slowly lift yourself up to the downward-facing dog. Hold this for a second and then step your right foot up between your hands and then bring your left knee to your mat. Make sure that you keep your hips square. Move your weight to your right foot so that your hips release to stretch the left front hip.

Reach your right hand up to the sky and bring the left hand to rest on the top of the left leg. This version is a great heart opener, and it stretches the front of your body. With each inhale, allow your chest to open more, and with each exhale, fall deeper into your backbend.

Make sure that you keep your heart open and picture a beautiful green color surrounding your chakra bringing in kindness and love. Stay here for a few more breaths and then slowly release. Step back into a downward-facing dog, and then bring your left foot forward and repeat on the other side.

1. Move into the easy pose for a chant.

Now, we are going to make sure that you can speak up and communicate. Chanting is a great way to bring alignment to your throat chakra.

Come out of the downward-facing dog and come to rest in an easy pose. Place your hands in Gyan Mudra. This is where your index fingers are touching your thumbs, and the other fingers are extended. Rest the back of your hands on your knees. Inhale so that your chest rises and your spine lengthens. Exhale, and allow your shoulders to relax.

Tuck your chin in towards your chest so that you create a throat lock. This will help to stimulate the throat. Start to chant "Hume Hum Brahm Hum." As you perform this chant, picture a blue light surrounding your throat. Watch as it gets rid of all of your doubts that you have regarding truth. Do this mantra three to 11 times.

1. Move into the dolphin pose.

Now, we are going to open up your intuition so that you can trust yourself and so you can have inner guidance. Dolphin pose will help to increase your facial circulation and the circulation of your brain.

Come up out of an easy pose and move to your hands and knees. Push yourself up into downward-facing dog. Lower the forearms so that they are on the ground. Make sure that you keep your elbows and shoulders in line. Move your hands so that your palms touch. Rock yourself forward so that your chin will move in front of your thumbs. Rock yourself back up to dolphin pose. Do this five to ten more times as you visualize an indigo light encircling your chakra. Once you have finished your movement, take a rest in child's pose.

1. Move into balancing butterfly

We're going to finish out this practice by opening up your trust and devotion. To perform this pose, you will need lots of concentration and balance.

Moving out of child's pose, kneel on your mat and tuck your toes under. Lift your knees up and move onto the balls of your feet. Make sure you keep your heels touching while they are under your hip bones, and then spread your knees open as wide as you can. You can rest your hands on the mat if you need it.

After you have stabilized yourself, bring your hands up to the heart center. If you want to raise the intensity, you can move your hands so that they are over your head. Hold this position.

While you are here, picture a line of energy moving from your root all the way through every chakra and exiting through your crown. The energy that comes out is a bright purple light that encircles your body. Stay here for five to ten breaths, and then slowly come out of the hold.

REIKI

Chakras and Reiki originated in different cultures, but they have lots of commonalities. There are a lot of reiki healers that will use the seven chakras. Reiki originated in Japan as a form of energy healing. A Buddhist monk, Mikao Usui, discovered it. He learned how to channel the energy that naturally flows through all of us. Everybody is able to use this energy.

Ever since reiki was first used, it used energy centers that let our prana move through the body. In the original tradition, they called these points tandens. Initially, reiki only focused on one tanden, known as the Sika tanden, which is found right below the belly button. But there are a total of three tandens. One is located in your upper chest, and another is in the center of the forehead.

Tandens are a different interpretation of chakras. They regulate energy flow. If tandens become blocked, energy is unable to flow through the body. Most people will go to a Reiki practitioner to have a Reiki treatment performed on them, but you can self-heal with Reiki with some practice.

Self-Healing Practice

1. Getting Ready

Find a quiet place where you won't be disturbed. Space should be as relaxing as possible. Turn the lights off and light some candles and play soothing reiki music. You want to get the environment ready for nurturing.

1. Kanji Hand Positions

Before you start your self-healing sessions, you need to center yourself by using the following three hand positions.

Position #1: You either sit or stand. Interlace your fingers and press the tips of your index fingers together. Shut your eyes and stay that way for about 30 seconds. Focus your energy on your solar plexus chakra.

Position #2: Like above, but this time, have your middle fingers touch. Picture your chakra filling up with healing white light.

Position #3: Drop your middle fingers so that all of the fingers are interlocked. Allow the energy in your chakra to spread freely through you.

. . .

Now, move into a comfortable position, either lying down or sitting. If you choose to lie down, put a pillow under your knees. If you feel a bit cold, cover up with a blanket.

1. Body Scan

Focus your attention on yourself and start to scan through your body. Begin on the top of your head and work your way down to your toes. Take a moment at each spot and think about what you feel there. If there is tension, release it. Is there any pain there? Are you able to accept the present moment? You are now centered and can move on the healing.

1. Point One

Put your hands over your face. The fingers should be pointed towards your forehead, and the sides of your hands should be touching. Hold this position for three minutes, or however long your body tells you it needs it.

1. Point Two

Move your hands to the top of your head so that your fingertips are touching. If you don't like this position, you can cup your hands over your ears. Again, hold for three minutes or longer.

1. Point Three

Move your hands to the back of your head. The bottom of the palms should cup the base of the skull. Hold for three minutes or more.

1. Point Four

Move your right hand so that it covers your throat. Place your left hand over the heart. Hold for three minutes or longer.

1. Point Five

Move your hands down to your shoulders and position them close to your neck. Hold for three minutes or more.

1. Point Six

Put your hands on your upper stomach with your fingers touching. They should rest just below the rib cage. Hold for three minutes or more.

1. Point Seven

Move your hands down so that they cover the belly button. Hold this for three minutes or more.

DEB LILITH

1. Point Eight

Slide your hands down so that they cover your lower belly just at the pubic bone. Hold this for three minutes or more.

1. Point Nine

Move your hands around to the lower back, keeping your fingertips touching like before. Hold this for three minutes or more.

1. Point Ten

Slide your hands down so that they cover the sacrum. Hold this for three minutes or more.

1. Point Eleven

Grab your left foot with both of your hands and hold this for three minutes or more.

1. Point Twelve

Now grab your right foot in both of your hands and hold this for three minutes or more.

1. Point Thirteen

Place your left foot into your left hand and your right foot into your right hand. Hold this for three minutes or more.

1. Point Thirteen(b)

Hold your feet in opposite hands and hold for three minutes or more.

While you are doing your self-healing practice, make sure that you stay comfortable while in each of the positions. If you aren't able to hold your feet, you can focus your energy on your feet and point your palms towards them. To help with chakra healing even more, focus on your chakras as you go through these moves.

MANTRAS

Mantras are basically a fancy word for an affirmation. Mantras are often used during mediations, or they become a meditation of their own. Sometimes, yoga practices will use mantras, as well. A lot of people who use mantras will use mala beads to help them. Most malas hold 108 beads because most mantra practices will tell you to repeat the mantra 108 times. 108 represents the mortal desires of man. There are some that only have 54, 27, or 18 beads. Many mala beads will have three extra beads that separate the beads into four sections, as well as a guru bead. The separator beads will have a different feel so that you know you can skip over it. Here are several mantras that you can try out to open up and heal your chakras. The first five are basic mantras that are known as seed mantras and help balance your energy.

1. OM
2. KRIM (kreem)
3. SHRIM (shreem)
4. HRIM (hreem)
5. HUM (hoom)
6. Root – "I am supported and strong."
7. Sacral – "I create my own reality."
8. Solar Plexus – "I deserve to follow my purpose and passion."
9. Heart – "I am open to receiving love, giving love. I am love."
10. Throat – "I am aligned with my truth. I speak with purpose."
11. Third Eye – "I am connected to my spirit and believe in my intuition."
12. Crown – "I am connected with the divine. I believe in the divine that surrounds me."
13. Root – LAM
14. Sacral – VAM
15. Solar Plexus – RAM
16. Heart – YAM
17. Throat – HAM
18. Third Eye – AUM
19. Crown – AH
20. Root – "I am at peace."
21. Sacral – "Creativity freely moves through my body."
22. Solar Plexus – "Letting go can be empowering."
23. Heart – "Giving is receiving."
24. Throat – "My words are my powers."
25. Third eye – "I am open."
26. Crown – "I surrender myself to the best that works

through me."

CHAKRA MEDITATIONS

Meditation gives you the power to transform your mind. It is meant to help positively change your emotions and to improve your concentration, and bring you a sense of calm. Through different meditation practices, you can train your mind to new patterns. With chakra meditations, you will be focusing your mind on your chakras to help clear them of blocked energies.

Root Chakra Meditation

This mediation is a tried-and-true method of creating a connection with your root chakra.

1. Find a comfortable position, either lying down or sitting, and take in three deep and slow breaths. Imagine the breath sending energy to your perineum; this is the space between your anus and genitals. With every exhale, release whatever you are holding in this area. This could be pain or fear. It could even be what you think you should feel while in this meditation.
2. Begin to gently tap at the top of your pubic bone or on either side of your hips' lower parts. This will wake up the connection you have with your root chakra.
3. As you continue to breathe in and out through your nose, direct your breath to your chakra. Picture a red glowing light growing and pulsing in your lower pubic area. For people who identify mostly as male, the light should spin

clockwise, and for people who identify mostly as female, the light should spin counterclockwise.
4. As you fall further into your meditative state, talk to your root chakra to see what it needs. Take some more breaths to notice if you get any feedback. This feedback could be a word, intuition, color, image, song, sound, or feeling. Act upon the feedback you receive. If nothing comes up, you don't need to worry about it. You will get something as you continue to practice.
5. If you didn't receive a message, but you start to feel a new awareness in your root chakra, something like a pulsating in the lower hips and down through your feet, you have made a connection to your root chakra.
6. As your meditation comes to a close, take three deep and slow breaths. Direct your inhales towards your feet so that you are grounded and then slowly open your eyes.
7. Make sure you take things slowly as you start out. This will take some time and practice, so be patient. If you end up feeling any sort of pain in your legs or lower back, you are trying too hard. Take a break and go back to it later. Remember that even seasoned meditators will sometimes find it hard to shut off their mind. Take this moment to observe these thoughts without judging them, and let them go, and gently refocus your mind.

Sacral Chakra Meditation

1. Find a comfortable position, either lying down or sitting, and take in three deep and slow breaths. With each inhale, imagine the breath sending energy to space right below your belly button. With every exhale, release whatever you

are holding in this area. This could be pain or fear. It could even be what you think you should feel while in this meditation. You can place your hand on this area while you meditate if you would like.
2. Begin to tap the area below your bellybutton with two fingers gently. You can also gently massage the area in a circular motion.
3. As you continue to breathe in and out through your nose, direct your breath to your chakra. Picture an orange glowing light growing and pulsing in your lower abdomen area. For people who identify mostly as male, the light should spin clockwise, and for people who identify mostly as female, the light should spin counterclockwise.
4. As you fall further into your meditative state, talk to your sacral chakra to see what it needs. Take some more breaths to notice if you get any feedback. This feedback could be a word, intuition, color, image, song, sound, or feeling. Act upon the feedback you receive. If nothing comes up, you don't need to worry about it. You will get something as you continue to practice.
5. If you didn't receive a message, but you start to feel a new awareness in your sacral chakra, something like a pulsating in this area, you have made a connection to your sacral chakra.
6. As your meditation comes to a close, take three deep and slow breaths. Direct your inhales towards your feet so that you are grounded and then slowly open your eyes.
7. Make sure you take things slowly as you start out. This will take some time and practice, so be patient. If you end up feeling any sort of pain in your lower abdomen, you are trying too hard. Take a break and go back to it later.

Solar Plexus Chakra Meditations

1. Find a comfortable position, either lying down or sitting, and take in three deep and slow breaths. With each inhale, imagine the breath sending energy to space right above your belly button. With every exhale, release whatever you are holding in this area. This could be pain or fear. It could even be what you think you should feel while in this meditation. You can place your hand on this area while you meditate if you would like.
2. Begin to gently tap the area above your belly button with two fingers. You can also gently massage the area in a circular motion.
3. As you continue to breathe in and out through your nose, direct your breath to your chakra. Picture a yellow glowing light growing and pulsing in your upper abdomen area. For people who identify mostly as male, the light should spin clockwise, and for people who identify mostly as female, the light should spin counterclockwise.
4. As you fall further into your meditative state, talk to your solar plexus chakra to see what it needs. Take some more breaths to notice if you get any feedback. This feedback could be a word, intuition, color, image, song, sound, or feeling. Act upon the feedback you receive. If nothing comes up, you don't need to worry about it. You will get something as you continue to practice.
5. If you didn't receive a message, but you start to feel a new awareness in your solar plexus chakra, something like a pulsating in this area, you have made a connection to your solar plexus chakra.
6. As your meditation comes to a close, take three deep and

slow breaths. Direct your inhales towards your feet so that you are grounded and then slowly open your eyes.
7. Make sure you take things slowly as you start out. This will take some time and practice, so be patient. If you end up feeling any sort of pain in your upper abdomen, you are trying too hard. Take a break and go back to it later.

Heart Chakra Meditation

1. Find a comfortable position, either lying down or sitting, and take in three deep and slow breaths. With each inhale, imagine the breath sending energy to the center of your chest. With every exhale, release whatever you are holding in this area. This could be pain or fear. It could even be what you think you should feel while in this meditation. You can place your hand on this area while you meditate if you would like.
2. Begin to tap your chest with two fingers gently. You can also gently massage the area in a circular motion.
3. As you continue to breathe in and out through your nose, direct your breath to your chakra. Picture a glowing green light growing and pulsing in your chest. For people who identify mostly as male, the light should spin clockwise, and for people who identify mostly as female, the light should spin counterclockwise.
4. As you fall further into your meditative state, talk to your heart chakra to see what it needs. Take some more breaths to notice if you get any feedback. This feedback could be a word, intuition, color, image, song, sound, or feeling. Act upon the feedback you receive. If nothing comes up, you

don't need to worry about it. You will get something as you continue to practice.
5. If you didn't receive a message, but you start to feel a new awareness in your heart chakra, something like a pulsating in this area, you have made a connection to your heart chakra.
6. As your meditation comes to a close, take three deep and slow breaths. Direct your inhales towards your feet so that you are grounded and then slowly open your eyes.
7. Make sure you take things slowly as you start out. This will take some time and practice, so be patient. If you end up noticing your heart is racing uncomfortably, you are trying too hard. Take a break and go back to it later.

Throat Chakra Meditation

1. Find a comfortable position, either lying down or sitting, and take in three deep and slow breaths. With each inhale, imagine the breath sending energy to the notch of your throat. With every exhale, release whatever you are holding in this area. This could be pain or fear. It could even be what you think you should feel while in this meditation.
2. Begin to gently tap the bone at the notch of your throat with two fingers. You can also gently massage the area in a circular motion.
3. As you continue to breathe in and out through your nose, direct your breath to your chakra. Picture a glowing blue light growing and pulsing in your throat. For people who identify mostly as male, the light should spin clockwise, and for people who identify mostly as female, the light should spin counterclockwise.
4. As you fall further into your meditative state, talk to your throat chakra to see what it needs. Take some more breaths

to notice if you get any feedback. This feedback could be a word, intuition, color, image, song, sound, or feeling. Act upon the feedback you receive. If nothing comes up, you don't need to worry about it. You will get something as you continue to practice.

5. If you didn't receive a message, but you start to feel a new awareness in your throat chakra, something like a pulsating in this area, you have made a connection to your throat chakra.

6. As your meditation comes to a close, take three deep and slow breaths. Direct your inhales towards your feet so that you are grounded and then slowly open your eyes.

7. Make sure you take things slowly as you start out. This will take some time and practice, so be patient. If you end up feeling any sort of pain in your neck, you are trying too hard. Take a break and go back to it later.

Third Eye Chakra Meditation

1. Find a comfortable position, either lying down or sitting, and take in three deep and slow breaths. With each inhale, imagine the breath sending energy to space between your brows. With every exhale, release whatever you are holding in this area. This could be pain or fear. It could even be what you think you should feel while in this meditation.

2. Begin to tap the area between your eyebrows with two fingers gently. You can also gently massage the area in a circular motion.

3. As you continue to breathe in and out through your nose, direct your breath to your chakra. Picture a glowing indigo light growing and pulsing in the area between your brows.

For people who identify mostly as male, the light should spin clockwise, and for people who identify mostly as female, the light should spin counterclockwise.

4. As you fall further into your meditative state, talk to your third eye chakra to see what it needs. Take some more breaths to notice if you get any feedback. This feedback could be a word, intuition, color, image, song, sound, or feeling. Act upon the feedback you receive. If nothing comes up, you don't need to worry about it. You will get something as you continue to practice.
5. If you didn't receive a message, but you start to feel a new awareness in your third eye chakra, something like a pulsating in this area, you have made a connection to your third eye chakra.
6. As your meditation comes to a close, take three deep and slow breaths. Direct your inhales towards your feet so that you are grounded and then slowly open your eyes.
7. Make sure you take things slowly as you start out. This will take some time and practice, so be patient. If you feel like you are getting a headache at the front of your head, you are trying too hard. Take a break and go back to it later.

Crown Chakra Meditation

1. Find a comfortable position, either lying down or sitting, and take in three deep and slow breaths. With each inhale, imagine the breath sending energy to the top of your head. With every exhale, release whatever you are holding in this area. This could be pain or fear. It could even be what you think you should feel while in this meditation.

2. Begin to tap the top of your head with two fingers gently. You can also gently massage the area in a circular motion.
3. As you continue to breathe in and out through your nose, direct your breath to your chakra. Picture a purple glowing light growing and pulsing at the top of your head. For people who identify mostly as male, the light should spin clockwise, and for people who identify mostly as female, the light should spin counterclockwise.
4. As you fall further into your meditative state, talk to your crown chakra to see what it needs. Take some more breaths to notice if you get any feedback. This feedback could be a word, intuition, color, image, song, sound, or feeling. Act upon the feedback you receive. If nothing comes up, you don't need to worry about it. You will get something as you continue to practice.
5. If you didn't receive a message, but you start to feel a new awareness in your crown chakra, something like a pulsating in this area, you have made a connection to your crown chakra.
6. As your meditation comes to a close, take three deep and slow breaths. Direct your inhales towards your feet so that you are grounded and then slowly open your eyes.
7. Make sure you take things slowly as you start out. This will take some time and practice, so be patient. If you end up feeling any sort of pain in your head, you are trying too hard. Take a break and go back to it later.

Multiple Chakra Meditation

1. Begin by laying down. While relaxing, try to direct a slow inhale towards your root chakra and slowly exhale the

energy through your mouth. Take three more breaths, and release anything that is stored in your root chakra. Get in touch with emotions that you may find in this chakra. You might even find a little bit of discomfort. Notice whatever is going on with her. Picture a red ball of light, healing your chakra. See if the initial sensations have changed.
2. Move up to your sacral chakra. Again, breathe into the chakra and release whatever is being held there. Notice any sensations or feelings. Visualize an orange ball of light healing your sacral chakra. Take note of any changes that happen in this chakra.
3. Turn your focus to the solar plexus chakra. Breathe into this chakra, noticing any sort of emotion or sensations. Picture a large yellow ball of light healing this chakra, and notice if you feel any changes.
4. Moving up to your heart chakra. Breathe into the chakra and take note of any sensations or emotions that live here. Image a large green ball of light healing this chakra. See if any changes happen.
5. Focus on your throat chakra now. Breathe healing energy into it and release anything that is there. Notice any sensations or feelings. Imagine a large blue light healing this chakra. Notice if any changes happen.
6. Slide up to your third eye chakra. Breathe into the chakra and notice any sensations or emotions that are here. Imagine a large indigo light healing this chakra. Take note of changes that happen.
7. Move up to your crown chakra. Breathe into your chakra and take note of any emotions or sensations that you are experiencing here. Picture a large purple light healing this chakra. Notice any changes that happen.
8. Take a moment to feel all of your chakras working together. Imagine a white light enveloping your body and healing

your chakras. Lie here for a few more minutes allowing the white light to heal your body. Once you feel you have meditated long enough, take three deep breaths, and slowly open your eyes.

Inner Vision

This meditation will require you to use your inner vision. Your words carry a vibration, and this imagery that you will picture will carry vibrations as well. You can use any type of image that brings your energy up. Test out a few images to see which will bring you sensations of hope, joy, and peace. To help you out, you can try imagining warm and golden sunlight. As you go through this mediation, your inner vision will likely start to show you things other than what we will go through. This is perfectly fine as long as it is uplifting.

1. Find a comfortable and quiet place where you can be undisturbed for a while. Close your eyes and take a moment to scan through your body to see if anything is uncomfortable. Take some time to get adjusted into a comfortable and supported position.
2. Turn your attention to your breath, but don't try to change it. You may still notice that it changes on its own. It could become slower and deeper. It could also become faster. Don't worry about what it's doing. Allow it to be. All you need to do is watch your breath and be fully aware of how it feels to breathe in and breathe out.
3. If your mind starts to wander during your meditation, bring it back to your breath. Don't get upset; just return to

your breath and how good it feels. Allow your breathing to relax.

4. Now that you're relaxed and focused on your breathing, picture yourself standing under the rays of a healing and warm golden light. This is a light of complete awareness. This is the essence of you and the essence of all living beings. It's all-encompassing love. It is the purest form of love. It is brighter than anything you have ever witnessed. It shines more than a million diamonds.

5. Allow this light to flow into your head and allow it to spread through your body at its will. Open yourself to the love that the light brings in. It has your best interests in mind and is clearing out whatever is keeping you from your truth and love. As this light spreads through you, it fills your tissues, organs, cells, and every part of your body. It spreads into your memories and thoughts and fills them with healing. It will allow you to learn from what you have been through.

6. This golden light pours through your crown chakra. It spreads into your third eye and opens up your connection to truth.

7. This warm and healing light flows down into your neck and through your throat chakra, balancing its energy and awakening your freedom. It spills over your shoulder and flows down your arms and into your wrists, hands, and fingers. It shoots through the ends of your fingers and flows back into the earth.

8. From your fifth chakra, the light slides down into your heart and fills you with love. It pools in your heart and flows out in every direction. It continues to travel down your chest, front, and back.

9. The light fills up your solar plexus and fills up your rib cage. This area touches your memories from your

childhood and adolescents and your experiences with parental figures. They are all made new and are provided love, softness, and space. You now know that a Divine Companion accompanied you in everything that you did. This could be a Guardian Angel, Jesus, Buddha, and Love, whatever you choose. This Presence has always been with you and still is with you through all of your challenges.

10. This light continues to fill every fiber of your being and all of your thoughts as it spills down into your sacral chakra. It embraces the child that is still living in you. The light tells your inner child that they are loved for who they are. Your inner child is told that they haven't done anything wrong. They only dreamed of the things they did. Your inner child is beautiful, whole, and complete. They are loved and safe.

11. The golden light continues to travel down into your root chakra and spills in all directions. The light opens up your awareness of your connections with the love of family and other people on Earth. This light is awakening your wisdom.

12. The light heals everything it touches. Everything in your body is being filled with the love of this light. The light flows down your legs and exits your feet, flowing into the Earth.

13. You are now filled with the flow of this pure light from the top of your head through the tips of your toes. Everything is being rinsed in this golden light on every level. Anything that doesn't serve you is being removed, leaving behind a warm and loving feeling. Relax and allow everything to be released.

14. Stay in this moment for five minutes or more.

15. As you are with this light, sense that you are the light. Notice as your body dissolves into the light. Notice the

freedom you feel of the light. You are unlimited and unbounded. Your creativity is unlimited because you are the light. You can do everything. You travel in every direction and are one with all beings.

Violet Flame

With this meditation, you can access fifth-dimensional frequencies that will help you to get rid of any unresolved and unhealed energies. This is an important thing to do when you want to clear out your chakras. Your chakras can't heal until you can heal from things that have happened to you. Things, good and bad, tend to hang around in our energy field. Until you can change the negative into light and love, you will suffer from chaos and negativity. The Violet flame can help you to change this. When you enter the fifth dimension, you will be connected to those you love, no matter where they are. You will also see that everybody is connected energetically as one. When you are here, your life will unfold through your passion because you will naturally choose what brings you joy.

1. Find a quiet space where you won't be disturbed, and get into a comfortable position. Sit so that your spine is straight, and your arms and legs are uncrossed. Your feet should be flat on the floor with your hands rested in your lap.
2. As you breathe in, imagine you are breathing in white light or love through your heart chakra. Stay with this for a moment until you are able to feel it. This works best when you feel you are devoted to forgiveness and love. If you are

finding this hard to do, try to think of a person who was kind to you. Find a memory of them and relax into their kind and warm energy. Take some time with this. Once you start to feel an opening, breathe the kindness out to somebody else. This will allow your heart chakra to open.

3. To start your meditation, begin with a decree like, "I am calling the violet flame to purify all that is inside of me." You can make your statement whatever you want as long as it starts with the words I AM. Repeat this statement a few times out loud and really notice your thoughts and feelings. It will work more powerfully if you can speak it out loud instead of saying it in your head. You need to stay in a forgiving and loving mindset. You can continue to repeat this phrase as often as you want.

4. Once you feel you are centered, you can begin to speak your violet flame meditation. This is very different from other meditation because you speak all the way through it. You can change this up however you would like.

5. "I am me. I am a presence. I breathe love into my heart. I am the center of the light. I call the complete power of the violet flame to change the memories, records, habits, effects, core, and causes of all of my actions, words, feelings, and thoughts I have ever used at any moment or in any dimension, unknown or known, that brings along any thought of…" (state what it is that you want to work on like prejudice, judgments, hatred, blame, anger, fear, belief in being bad, shame, self-hate, power misuse, misuse of energy, disease, suffering, powerlessness, victimhood, or poverty.)

6. "With my intention as love and forgiveness, I burn the violet flame through every particle and wave of my life energy in every time and place that reflects anything less than what serves my true, positive purpose."

7. "I trust Source to change every part of me on every single level into the highest level of light and love and abundance and health."
8. "I ask that I fill my presence with the golden light of love, abundance, and health."
9. "In my creator's name, I accept this as done. So it is."

Boat of Wellbeing

1. Go to a quiet place that you like being, where you are able to relax fully, and you know you won't be disturbed. Turn off your phone. Get into a comfortable seated or lying position, if you can do so without going to sleep.
2. Make sure that you are comfortable and then shut your eyes. Focus your attention on your breath. Don't try to do anything to it; just notice it. Your breath is going to change just by focusing on it naturally. Your body and mind will start to relax.
3. You will likely notice tension being released from your body. You could feel as if you are sinking. Like gravity is pulling you into a sense of relaxation. Continue to focus on your breath. Breathe in. Breathe out in and out.
4. Take a slow scan across your body to see if you are holding anything inside of your mind or body. There may be something you have been dealing with that thoughts come up about it. You may notice that you have tightness or tension within your body, which means that you are grasping or reaching for something.
5. As you take note of these grasps and stresses, allow them to leave. If you need to attend to something in your life, it can wait and be worked on later. This is a time to relax, to

take a little vacation from having to think or plan. If you do notice some stress, don't but blame it on anybody else. Notice that it is there and then allow it to go.

6. Picture yourself resting on a comfy boat that is floating gently down the river of rejuvenation and love. You can create any type of boat that you want. This boat is being guided by your heart, which has aligned itself with abundance.

7. The boat has resonated on every level with your pure heart. Everything on the boat is everything that you will need.

8. When you need something, it will show up in front of you. You have loving companions to take the journey with you. You have all the best food that you will need to nourish you. There is music playing that soothes you—everything the boat brings you well-being and joy.

9. The only thing you need to do is enjoy yourself and relax and notice everything that you have in your life. Everything is under control. There are no cares or concerns in your life right now because you have everything you need. There is no need to ask for anything. When you notice you need something, it will show up, no matter what it is.

10. When you notice that you want to do something, or fix something, relax and know that it has already been taken care of. This is your dream vacation, where somebody else is taking care of everything.

11. There is no need to come up with any plans for how to get things. All you have to do is relax and know that your boat will take you where you need to travel, and it will happen in the best way possible.

12. Allow yourself to relax because everything is being taken care of. Focus on the healing and nurturing that is available to you. As you float on down the river, you are being taken further into relaxation and wellbeing. You are filled with

clarity and light. Everything good is here. All you have to do is let the river take you into love. Everything is completely taken care of.
13. If stress starts to rise up, don't try to control it. Notice that it's there, and remind yourself that everything is being taken care of. Relax into the love that surrounds you. Allow your knots to be untangled. Everything is healed. You are at home, nurtured, loved, and appreciated. You are done with work and can relax. You don't have to do anything. Everything is being done for you.
14. An entire staff of beings is on the boat with you to take care of whatever you need. When you need something, one of these beings appears to help you.
15. Allow yourself to float along and surrender yourself to a delicious relaxation.
16. Once you feel ready, you can open your eyes and have a look around. How did it feel? Was it hard for you to let things go and allow other people to take care of the things you needed? If you did, you're not the only person that has that struggle.
17. Were you able to feel any sense of relief in trusting that you were traveling along the right course that everything had been handled? Were you able to feel the loving energy healing you? This is what you want to reach.
18. The more you can feel this is you, the higher you will vibrate, and the cleaner your chakras will be. The more you vibrate at this level, the healthier and more connected to your true self you will become.

Chakra Healing

This meditation script will bring you along on a relaxing trip that will restore and cleanse your chakra's energy. Your entire energy system will retire into a state of balance and harmony.

1. Let your eyes slowly close. Focus on your breath and allow it to move down through your body, allowing it to relax your belly and soften the mind.
2. Feel how your seat below you supports you and connects you with the ground beneath you. Allow it to take on your full weight.
3. Notice all of the sounds that are around you and allow them to be there. Notice the light that you can see through your closed lights. Feel the air that touches your body since the sky that is above and the Earth that stretches out all around you.
4. Let your mind become empty of anything that you don't need to hold onto. Let this go away and flow out. Let your body release anything that it doesn't currently need. Let this go away and flow out.
5. Pull yourself out of the experiences that you have gone through today. Pull your energies back to your center. Allow yourself to be grounded at the moment.
6. Start to sense what is around you. Inhale with the energy, and notice the rise and fall of your breathing. The way it comes and goes. How it sounds, feels, and its temperature.
7. Take a deep breath in, all the way down to where your body rests, just below your spine, at your root chakra. Your belonging. Breathe in here. Allow this space to expand and soften gently. Let it take in nourishment and your energy.

8. Let you become connected to the ground below you, deep into the depths of the Earth. Bring in the color red. Allow your root chakra to become bathed in this red color, empowering and grounding you. You are in the here and now. Allow your root chakra to take in everything that it needs.
9. Once you feel you are ready, let your awareness come to your belly, right below the belly button. Your sacral chakra. The center of emotional intelligence, pleasure, and creativity.
10. Breathe into this space and allow it to expand and soften with your breath. Allow it to take in energy and nourishment. Bring in the color orange. Allow your sacral to be wrapped in this color. Let it feed on power.
11. Once you are ready, move on up to the area just below your breastbone. Your solar plexus. Your power.
12. Breathe into this area and let the solar plexus to expand and soften with your breath. Bring in the bright color yellow. Let your chakra be surrounded by this sunshine. It will nurture and replenish your chakra. Allow your chakra to take whatever it needs.
13. Once you feel you are ready, move your awareness to the middle of your chest. Your heart. Your space of love and development.
14. Breathe gently into your heart and allow it to expand and soften. Bring in the color green into this space. Allow your heart to be surrounded by this nourishment and healing. Allow your heart to consume whatever energy it needs to while you are here.
15. When the time is right, move your awareness to your neck. Your throat. Where your will and expression live.
16. Breathe as the chakra softens and expands. Bring in the color of the sky. As the throat is coated in the blue, allow it

to soften, open, and clear. Allow it to open so that you are free to express yourself. Allow your throat to take in everything that it needs.

17. Once you are ready, bring your focus up to your forehead to your third eye. Your chakra of intuition and wisdom. Let this area expand and soften.
18. Bring in the color of indigo—the beautiful color of the night sky. Allow your third eye to be wrapped in this color, bringing balance and insight into your third eye. Allow your chakra to take whatever it needs.
19. In your time, move up to your head. To the crown chakra. To your oneness.
20. Bring in the color purple to caress your chakra. Notice as it restores and balances your crown. Allow it to take in everything that it needs.
21. Once you feel ready to return to yourself and become whole, back to the rise and fall of your breathing, back into you, take a breath into your core. To yourself, say, "I am perfect and whole."
22. Let these words bathe you in their energy. Let it sweep across your spirit, emotions, mind, and body. Take in all the energy that you need.
23. In your own perfect time, start to notice the air that touches your body. Take note of the sounds that are close and far away.
24. Take a moment to close down your chakras a bit. Having the intention to do so is enough. Notice the support that you have below you. Notice the way it makes you feel. Support yourself with kindness and love for the unique human being that you are.
25. Once you feel ready, slowly move your toes and fingers and gently open your eyes.

White Light

Performing this healing meditation regularly will help to increase your self-awareness. This will unlock your ability to naturally heal and will improve your wellbeing. This meditation can be used for yourself and for the entire planet as well. This is the perfect way to begin your day.

1. Begin by sitting in a comfortable chair that fully supports your back and body. Allow your eyes to close. Start to notice your breathing. Don't try to make any changes; just observe how it feels as you breathe in and out. Do this for a few minutes.
2. Imagine a stream of white light flowing down for your source and through the top of your head in your crown chakra. This is a glorious waterfall of love, joy, and wellbeing that is coming straight from your creator.
3. This light shines brightly and shows every color in the rainbow. Every color carries a specific healing power and brings nourishment to every part of your being.
4. Breathe this stream of light into your crown chakra. This light flows into every cell of your body and brings you enlightenment, and nurtures you.
5. Breathe this white light all the way through your body until it exits the soles of your feet and spreads deep into Mother Earth.
6. You are creating a continuous and permanent line of light coming from your source all the way down through your very being into Earth. As you breathe out, you breathe in

another dose of this white light and its healing energy, and it goes out to every person in the world.

7. This beautiful light circulates you, and you are free to surrender and let go of everything that ever kept you from true love. Any old residues of energy have been taken over by this white light. They immediately disappear in its brilliance.
8. From your crown chakra, you breathe in this perfect light through to your third eye, located in the middle of your forehead. You breathe in pure clarity and love. You release all that has blocked you from receiving the highest amount of love possible.
9. You ask this healing white light to open up your inner vision to broaden so that your perspective expands.
10. Through your crown chakra, you breathe in more of this healing light and send it through to your throat chakra, living at the base of the throat. This is where your truth and ability to speak comes from. This will release everything that covers your truth.
11. The light flows out of your energy center and affirms to the world around that you the highest truth of yourself. When you breathe out, this pure light flows out of your throat chakra out to everybody and brings love and healing to the entire world with your voice.
12. You breathe in more of this white light through your crown and send it deep into your heart chakra. This expands your heart into the beautiful light and sends it out in all directions.
13. You are a unified being of pure light, and you are breathing in healing light into and through and all-around your body. Through this healing, you release whatever has kept you from love. You have become united with this light. When

you breathe out, you are sending this healing light to humanity through your heart.
14. As you breathe in more light through your crown, you send it down to your solar plexus. This is your parent chakra. This frees you of all of your soul and the rules that you have created that covers your light and love.
15. You are expanding into this unified pure light field, and you are breathing this light into every part of your body.
16. As you breathe in more light, you send the light down to your sacral chakra. Your child chakra.
17. You can feel an innocent child living within you. This pure light sends compassion and love to this child who resides inside of you. This opens you up to Source so that you feel that you're loved.
18. You surrender all the things that cover your light. You have become a unified being, a pure light. You breathe the healing nature of the light into and around you.
19. Through your crown, you send more light down to your root chakra. This is where you feel your tribal connection with the Earth and all other human beings.
20. You release any constricting and separating beliefs that you have stored in this area. You have allowed yourself to become one with the pure light. The white light is now coursing through you and around you.
21. With every breath you take, this light expands out into a sphere of light that encapsulates your physical body. It includes the alpha and omega chakras that live above and below your body.
22. You let go of everything that vibrates lower than is healthy.
23. You have become the pure and beautiful light that lives within and around your body. Through your heart, you breathe out this brilliance to everybody.
24. Every breath you breathe in expands this light. This light

has now reached your emotional body. This light floods all the way through your emotions and cleanses everything.
25. You release whatever lives inside of your emotional body that is keeping you from your light. You are one with this light on every level of your being. With every exhale, you send this diamond light out to all humankind through your heart. You have become the conduit for this light.
26. You continue to expand this light out into your casual body.
27. This healing light is now changing every memory, record, habit, effect, core, and cause that was created by any action you have taken in any dimension that has created a limitation.
28. The healing light is changing every cell of your energy that shows anything less than infinite perfection.
29. You fill every area with your white light. You are connected with this light and sending it out to every single human being.
30. Your white light continues to expand out to your mental body and permeates through all of your thoughts.
31. You release all of your limiting beliefs. You are one with this healing light.
32. On your next breath, you expand the light out to your etheric body and permeates through to all of the subtle energies. You release any limiting energetic connections.
33. You are one with this healing light. You send out this healing light out to everybody through your heart.
34. With your next breath, your light will expand out to your spiritual body.
35. You are becoming one with this light more and more. With each exhale, you send more energy out to the world around you.
36. With your next inhale, your light spreads out to your

avatar self. You send powerful light out to everybody, connecting more with the light.

37. With your next inhale, you connect with the divine feminine and masculine rays. They merge as one within you. They bring you forgiveness and fill your entire being.
38. Through your heart, you send these rays out to all humankind, helping them heal all old wounds.
39. Everything that is not serving your higher purpose is released, sending you into a state of love and light.
40. You are a continuous and connected field of healing light that completely encircles and fills every layer of you in all dimensions. Through your heart, out into every dimension, you send out the healing power of this light.
41. This power and light will permanently radiate through your heat and fill all areas of your being. It will always shine out to everybody in the world so that they can enjoy this healing light.
42. You will radiate this healing light throughout your day. You are the unity of spirit. This healing field will guide you in everything that you do. The light has become anchored in your heart.
43. Through gratitude and humility, you will now have the healing light shine through you to everybody so that you are a channel for the highest of healing, light, and love.
44. You are the light of healing. You're led by the purest light. So it is.

WHAT COULD BE SLOWING YOU DOWN

YOU HAVE BEEN WORKING HARD to get your chakras healed, but it seems like no matter how hard you try, nothing is changing. There are lots of different things that can keep you from opening your chakras, but we are going to look at the seven most common holdbacks.

Fear

The first thing that can hold you back is fear. Ironically, experiencing fear is also a symptom of a blocked root chakra. Fear does serve a purpose in life. It helped our ancestors to survive because it alerts you to danger, but when you let yourself constantly fear things, your fear will dictate what you do. This will end up closing you off to life, and you will end up feeling as if you have run out of options. With chronic fear, you will end up believing that you can't survive.

The best way to beat this fear is to face it. As you start facing your fears, you will create a track record. Eventually, you will see that you can deal with loss and pain. You will come to realize that what you fear isn't actually all that bad.

Addiction

People will typically develop an addiction to try and make themselves feel good. When the solar plexus chakra is blocked, you lose that good feeling, so you try to seek it elsewhere. When you don't feel good, you will likely experience guilt or shame. Your addiction will help you to "feel good" and help to ease those negative feelings. But, when that addiction wears off, all of those negative feelings come rushing back in and will likely be stronger.

Low Self-Esteem

This goes hand in hand with the previous problem. This tends to be where the shame originates. Because you don't feel okay, you start to think you are useless and can't do anything for yourself. Or you feel that anything you do won't fix anything, and everything is just going to remain lousy.

To fix this problem, do the same thing you did to fix your addiction. You have to decide that you are loved and worth everything. Once you make this conscious decision, you will quit owning all the negativity that happens. You won't believe that you deserve all of those bad moments. Unconsciously, you will begin to make more positive moments because you will reject the negative ones.

Grief

This doesn't have to be grief over a loved one. That's perfectly normal and will usually pass once you have worked through your loss. Any time you lose something you could feel some form of grief. This is a natural response, but if it turns into chronic grief, it could end up causing you to become stuck in bitterness or anger.

All of this will keep you from creating a relationship or maintaining one that you already have.

When you do experience loss, take some time to reorganize your life so that you can move forward. You can't let your life center on the loss or the grief.

Can't Communicate

By communicate, I mean telling the truth. A partial truth still makes it a lie. Some people are only able to communicate partially, others can't communicate at all. It is important that you focus on your words, and you should make a conscious effort to make sure that what you say is clearly understood. It's not the other person's job to understand what you say; you need to say it to make sure they understand.

Illusion

Illusion is the opposite of insight. Illusion means that you see things only with your physical senses. This prevents you from being able to see everything. When you see blood, all you see is a red liquid. When it is magnified, you would see the platelets and red and white cells that make up your blood. Think about this, if you were blindfolded and your ears plugged, why is it that you can still sense that someone is close to you.

When you don't consider the intentions of other people, you will likely misunderstand the things they do. This is what causes an illusion. Problems will come up when you take those illusions at face value.

Attachments

People can have attachments to just about anything: food, sex, money. Having something is very different than being attached to it. You can have money because you need it to purchase things you need to survive. But if you desire to obtain more of it, and it starts to dictate the things you do, this becomes greed. You should enjoy what you have and your relationships, but you should feel as if you can't live without it.

OPENING THE THIRD EYE

ONCE YOU HAVE your third eye completely opened, your wisdom and intuition will come alive as well. For most people, opening the third eye chakra can be a challenge, but for others, it might be completely out of their reach.

When you have stimulated your third eye, you will be able to see how your previous decisions have influenced your life and how present decisions will affect your future. You will develop mental flexibility so that you can see the difference between what something seems to be and what it actually is. With the help of your sixth chakra, you will be able to move past your normal abilities. The following strategies can help you open your third eye chakra.

Get Grounded

. . .

The first thing you need to be able to do before you can open your third eye is to have your feet grounded. Also, it is important to go at this slowly and create a good foundation that will give you a good amount of discernment so that you can read your new perceptions with clarity.

Grounding is important because you need to have plenty of energy coursing through your energy system to help support a healthy opening. Once you have activated your third eye, the information you get will likely seem unusual and possibly even disturbing.

When you have enough energy and are grounded, you will be able to expand yourself into these new perceptions. This will allow you to avoid common negative side effects of a third eye awakening, like confusion.

Create Silence

It is important that you learn how to have silence in your mind. This can be accomplished through meditation, sitting quietly by yourself, or allowing yourself to be lost in your favorite sport or art.

This helps because your third eye will bring your senses to new levels. Many people will refer to this as "the space in between," or psychic abilities. In order to listen to the information you are sent through your third eye, you have to be able to hear a whisper. If you have a busy mind, you will likely miss your messages.

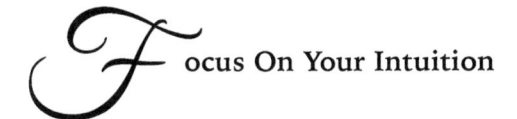

Focus On Your Intuition

There are many different ways that you can improve your intuition. Since your third eye is your center of wisdom and vision, then it helps to get to know your dreams and what they mean. You may even want to try out lucid dreaming or try reading tarot cards. Find different ways to use your intuition during your day.

Since your third eye is where your higher perception levels live, it helps to be more tuned in to your intuition. You don't have to be perfect at intuition. All you need to do is be curious and learn more about intuitive techniques. After some practice, these techniques will become familiar, and you will be confident in your abilities.

The great thing is, there's no need to be serious about it. You can have fun and explore things so that you can keep your chakras open to wonder.

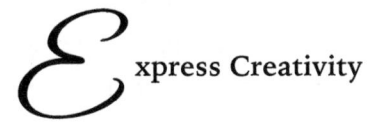

Express Creativity

. . .

Allow your creativity to really flow by using activities that will allow your imagination to let loose. For example, try learning something new. Don't worry about being perfect either. Allow your inspiration to control your hands and be open to whatever results you get.

Creativity is a perfect way to allow your rational mind to loosen up. All of that mental chatter that tells you that something is wrong or right, and that likes to control every little thing that you do, it will be silenced with creativity.

When you are able to silence this area of your mind, and you use all of the possibilities that are available to you, your third eye will start to blossom.

Chanting

Chanting a mantra will help you to listen to yourself. You can repeat the seed sound for the third eye chakra, AUM, as long as you can keep your focus. You can choose some of the words that I will list below to create your own manta. Pick what works best for you. Repeat them in rhythm with your breath while meditating. You can also repeat them to yourself during the day in a japa fashion. It should become one with your consciousness.

- SHOHAMSO (seo-ha-hm)

- HAMSA (ha-hm-saw)
- VIJNANA (veez-hn-ya-nah)

To help you connect even more with your third eye, you can follow these extra tips. These are all great ways to improve your intuition and energy.

- Work with your spirit guides
- Grow psychic awareness
- Cultivate curiosity about symbols
- Practice contemplation
- Practice contemplation
- Focus on the space "in between" things
- Practice intuition
- Allow your imagination freedom
- Meditate under the moon
- Guided meditations
- Allow yourself to be comfortable in silence
- Visualization
- Strengthen your root and throat chakras
- Practice divination
- Dream interpretation and lucid dreaming

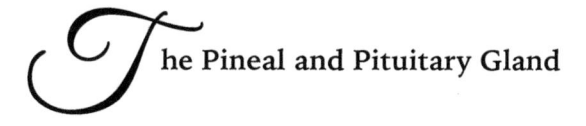

The Pineal and Pituitary Gland

. . .

If you look up information about the third eye, you will likely start seeing information about the pineal and pituitary gland. Glands and chakras tend to have an intimate relationship because they all represent bodily functions. The pituitary gland is the "master gland" because it is in control of the majority of other glands as well as the production of hormones.

The pineal gland is found in the middle of your brain and is in line with your eyes. Yogic traditions see this gland as the seat of the soul and are the source of psychic abilities. The pineal gland produces melatonin and regulates our sex maturation and sleep cycle. To help awaken your third eye, you need to nurture your pineal gland. Here is how you can help your pineal gland:

- Spend some time in total darkness because this can stimulate the pineal gland and can produce what is needed to correct the hormones.
- Meditate because it can balance the nervous system's activities and stimulates various areas of the brain.
- Take supplements and eat foods that support a healthy pineal gland, like tamarind fruit, apple cider, and iodine.
- Get plenty of natural light.

Obstacles

. . .

Many people will run into some problems when trying to open their third eye. These are some of the most common problems.

- They listen to others through their own concerns
- They tend to descend consciousness, are conceited
- They get distracted by details
- Their ego is attached to powers
- They have self-deceiving truths
- They communicate on the surface
- They aren't dreamy
- They use information about others for their own personal gain
- Ignores what their body tells them
- They do foolish things
- They are rigidly rational
- They see others as different

If you can overcome these issues and follow the techniques explained above, you will be able to open your third eye and experience life in a new light.

COMMONLY ASKED QUESTIONS

To finish this book, we are going to go over some common questions concerning chakras just to make sure that you have a great understanding of them.

What Are Chakras?

Chakras are the energy centers in the body that sends, receives, and uses information about different things of your being. In Sanskrit, chakra translates to wheel. This is the perfect name for the energy centers since they move in a circular motion.

How Many Chakras Do We Have?

There are many different thoughts about this question, but most people acknowledge that there are seven main chakras.

Do Women and Men Have the Same Chakras?

Yes, every human being's chakras work the same. But, chakras one, three, and five do have masculine qualities while two, four, and six have feminine qualities. Because of this, men will often have stronger chakras that have masculine qualities, while women will be stronger with the feminine ones. There are some exceptions, though.

How Can Chakras Affect My Life?

Chakras affect every part of our lives. Your DNA holds your biological information and genetics, and your chakras hold the information for your energy. If there are parts of your life that you want to make better, beginning with your chakras is a great place to begin.

Where Are the Chakras Located and Related?

- The root chakra is located at the tailbone and relates to vitality, grounding, and prosperity.
- The sacral chakra is located at the pelvis and relates to intimacy, sexuality, and fertility.
- The solar plexus chakra is located right above the belly button and relates to energy, mental clarity, and confidence.
- The heart chakra is located at the heart and relates to love and compassion.
- The throat chakra is located at the throat and relates to truth, artistry, and communication.
- The third eye chakra is located in the middle of your forehead, right between your eyebrows, and relates to intuition, dreams, and vision.
- The crown chakra is located at the top of the head and relates to unity, wisdom, and intelligence.

Will One Blocked Chakra Affect All The Others?

Yes, because they all work together. Just like a piece of jewelry, they are tied together and have energy currents that move up and down the body. When one is blocked, the chakras located right above and right below the blocked one are affected because it keeps energy from freely flowing.

Can I Feel Them?

Most people can feel them. Inside your body, your third chakra might feel like butterflies in your belly. You might feel a warm sensation near your heart that tells you that your fourth chakra is working. On the outside of your body, if you place your hand over one of the chakras, you might feel something similar to a pillow of energy. Ask a good friend to lay down and then put your hand over their fourth or third chakra. Hover your hand about two feet above each point, and then slowly move your hand closer to their body until you can feel their energy touching yours. You will notice that it feels similar to a cushion.

CONCLUSION

Thank you for making it through to the end of the book; let's hope it was informative and able to provide you with all of the tools you need to achieve your goals, whatever they may be.

The next step is to start working with chakras. An easy way to start connecting with them and opening them up is to start meditating. It doesn't need to be anything fancy or chakra driven at first. Getting use to the basic idea of meditation will help you out later. Once you feel you have that down, you can start using meditations that are aimed towards your chakras. You can also try out the other methods for opening your chakras like yoga, mantras, and reiki. Take this process slow as opening them too quickly can cause side effects that are less than pleasant. Appreciate the process, and don't try to rush things. They will progress as they need to.

BUDDHISM

An In-depth Guide for Beginners

DEB LILITH

Copyright © 2020 by Deb Lillith

All rights reserved.

No part of this book may be reproduced in any form or by any electronic or mechanical means, including information storage and retrieval systems, without written permission from the author, except for the use of brief quotations in a book review.

INTRODUCTION

Thank you for choosing this book, and congratulations on taking a step towards bringing Buddhism into your life. This book is filled with information about Buddhism, its beliefs, and how it came to be.

Buddhism is a complex religion and spiritual following. There are many offshoots of the Buddhist faith throughout various Asian countries. Still, most of their teachings are the same or at least very similar.

The first thing that we will go over in this book is the origins of Buddhism. In this chapter, you will learn how Buddhism got its start. We will be looking at the life and lessons of Siddhartha Gautama, which ultimately became Buddhism. We'll then move into the teachings and principles of Buddhism. This will go over all of its fundamental beliefs, including the eightfold path and dharma. This is a very important chapter that will help you out the most if you are thinking about becoming a Buddhist. After that, we are going to look at the importance of numbers in the Buddhist

INTRODUCTION

faith. Numbers play a huge role in Buddhism, including the five precepts and the four noble truths.

We will then make our way into the Buddhist perfections. The perfections are separated out into two groups. One is the Mahayana, and the other is the Theravada. In total, we will be going over 16 perfections. Then we will discuss the idea of karma. This will explain what karma is and how you can affect your karma. We'll also talk about rebirth. Rebirth is a pretty important concept of the Buddhist faith, and it's important to understand what it means. Lastly, we will go over how you bring Buddhism into your life. Whether you plan on being a Buddhist or just want to bring some of the Buddhist energy into your life, these practices can help you.

Before we get started, I would like to ask you to please leave a review if you find this information helpful!

THE ORIGINS OF BUDDHISM

ONE OF THE biggest beliefs for Buddhism is that anybody has the ability to reach higher conditions in the universe and the world. When and where did Buddhism start? What made it so popular and caused it to capture the minds and hearts of millions of people all around the world?

IT ALL STARTED WITH THE MIRACLE OF LIFE

For all Buddhists, the teachings and life of Siddhartha Gautama are what give them their core values and ideals that they follow within the community and faith. Buddhism was created during the late sixth century BCE by a man called Siddhartha Gautama, or the Buddha. This became the most important religion for most of the Asian countries. Buddhism has taken on many forms, but everyone has tried to draw from Buddha's experiences, teachings, and the essence of his teachings. We didn't have a good account of his life until Ashvaghosa wrote about Buddha Charita in the first of the second century CE.

. . .

Somewhere near 560 BCE, Prince Siddhartha Gautama was born. He was to be the heir of the Royal Shakya clan to rule over a kingdom called Lumbini that was located at the foothills of the Himalayan Mountains. This kingdom was farther than Brahmanic land in the Gangetic Plains. His teachings were intellectual, spiritual, and focused on change. During this time, Hindu ideals were about rejecting social and family life by anyone who was seeking the Truth. These can be viewed as moving away from the Vedic fire sacrifices.

Prince Siddhartha's conception was pure. His gestation period was not filled with violence, and his birth was a miracle. The soles of his feet, his palms, and fingerprints had signs that told him he was to be either a universal conqueror or savior known as "Lord of the Four Quarters." He would soon become their savior, and the people who had followed him would become India's emperors. Siddhartha Gautama was a warrior son of the queen and king. Legend has it that when he was born, a prophet predicted that he could become a renouncer and withdraw from his royal life. In order to keep this from happening, his parents gave him all the pleasures and luxuries in life. They raised him in what they thought was a perfect world by making sure he never knew sorrow. He mastered all pleasures and arts. When he was 16, he was quickly married to his beautiful, pure, and royal cousin, and it wasn't long after that they had a son. As was predicted at his birth, the gods had decided to make sure that he rose above the need for pleasure by showing him all of the sufferings that humans have to deal with in the real world.

LEAVING A PLEASURABLE LIFE

There are many similarities between Siddhartha's teachings and lives, who became the Buddhist and the Jain teacher, Mahavira. Siddhartha was also known as the Enlightened One, and he became the epitome of all Buddhists. These two men lived simultaneously; both of them were from North India and Kshatriya by birth. They both would end up rejecting dharma along with the Brahmin's authority. Siddhartha Gautama and Mahavira left their homes during their 30s to find a higher path that would lead them to Nirvana.

When he became a young man, he took four chariot rides where he saw all the different types of human suffering: old age, illnesses, and death along with a renouncer. Seeing all these contrasts between the life that he was used to and all this suffering made him see that all of life's pleasures only masked human sufferings.

He saw a white-haired old man, bent over, frail, and only had a few teeth left during the first ride. Siddhartha was shocked as this was the first time he had ever seen an old person. The gods told him that this was what all men went through in their lives, and he, too, would go through this.

On his second ride, he saw a man who had a high fever and was covered in boils. Siddhartha tried to understand this sight, too. He took another ride and saw a dead body being carried by grieving relatives to be cremated. Last, he saw a wandering beggar who was trying to get rid of the pains that he felt due simply to his existence. It was these sights that helped him make the decisions to leave the palace pleasures.

He decided to leave his wife and son. He left behind all of his belongings. He cut all of his hair off. He took some ascetic teachers with him and did a severe form of renunciation in a forest until he almost starved himself to death. He realized that all this fasting was only causing more pain and suffering, and he could no longer concentrate on anything. Some legends say he went six months living this way; others say it was six years. It really doesn't matter. All that matters is he rejected the severe teachings of these men. He finally realized that they were only adding to his painful frustrations and not leading him to salvation. He started eating again, and as his body got stronger, he started meditating on the universe and humanity's nature. Legend states that the death god tried his best to prevent him from performing his meditations. He found shelter under a fig tree and resumed his meditation. By the next morning, he had attained Nirvana or enlightenment. This sacred fig tree was located in Gaya. Once he had reached Nirvana, he received the true answers for why people had to suffer and a complete release from them.

Some of his devoted followers say this same tree still grows at the exact place, but they now refer to it as Bodh Gaya. Of course, as with the way of the world, there are skeptics who say that it could not possibly be the same exact tree because there is no way that a tree could survive for more than 2500 years. What is more believable is that there is still a fig tree growing at this place, but it is from seedlings that have grown from the original tree. If you ever get the chance to go to Bodh Gaya, you will encounter people who will try to sell you a 'real leaf' from that original fig tree. Many visitors and Buddhists return with one of these relics.

AN ENLIGHTENED BUDDHA

From this point on, he began teaching others about these truths because he was worried about their sufferings. During his first sermon, he talked about the "Four Noble Truths" and the "Eight-Fold Path" that would end up becoming the center of Buddhism. We will cover the Eight Fold Path in another chapter. For now, let's look at the "Four Noble Truths." The first of these truths teach us that there will be suffering during life. We normally live our lives full of all the pains and pleasures of our mind and body. He said that pleasures would never give you lasting happiness. These will always be tied to suffering because we suffer when we want them. We suffer because we want them to continue. We suffer because we want the pain to go away so that pleasure can come to us. The second Noble Truth shows us that our suffering happens because of our sensual desires and our attachment to the world.

We crave for things not to be as they are and a sense of pleasure. We don't like accepting our lives. The Third Noble Truth tells us that there is an end to our suffering. If we can withdraw from our senses, desires, and attachments, this suffering will disappear. The fourth Noble Truth gives us a way to find that end. This truth shows us the 'Middle Way' that rejects both extremes of abstinence and pleasure. You can find these by following the 'Eight-Fold Path and the Middle Way.' If you can follow these combined paths, you will attain Nirvana, which is a state of all-knowing, lucid awareness where there is nothing but joy and peace.

. . .

The "Eight-Fold Path" is usually shown as a wheel with eight spokes. These spokes represent:

- Right Concentrations or Meditations
- Right Mindfulness or being present in every moment
- Right Endeavors
- Right Livelihood or Occupation
- Right Actions
- Right Speech
- Right Intentions
- Right Views

If a person can live these perfectly, you could reach Nirvana or the absolute peace beyond all sufferings and desires. The Middle Way shows how we can reject every extreme lifestyle, action, emotion, and thought. Instead of living a life of indulging in intense pleasures, Buddha advocates for a more balanced lifestyle of balance and cultivating emotional and mental calmness through morality and meditation.

For the remainder of Buddha's life, and up until the day he died at the age of 80 in 480 BCE, he taught and lived by these ideas. There were two armies from rival kingdoms in India who were getting ready for war. Buddha stepped in and taught them about nonviolence. He, and those who would soon be known as his followers, spent their time explaining and expanding on all of the truths' meanings and came up with all of the information that people needed to ensure that they traveled the Middle Way. These early teachings that the original people of Buddhism wrote about were all written in Pali, which, at that time, was the main language that the people spoke in North India. These first writings were not written in the Brahmin preserved archaic Vedic Sanskrit. These earlier Buddhists would often use the Pali term of dhamma instead of the Sanskrit word dharma, describing the Middle Way as the best code of conduct that all humans and everything universal needs to live by.

A LOYAL FOLLOWING BEGINS

As more and more people followed Buddha, he began organizing monastic orders. They had to shave their heads, renounce their possessions and family, living a nonviolent life without being attached or desiring anything. They only ate food that had been donated. They had to wear robes that were the color of saffron. They had to wander for eight months out of the year, and after that, they could live in a monastery during the monsoon months.

Buddhism has three gems: Buddha, dharma, and sangha. The early accounts state that Buddha would only accept men into the sangha. After some women appealed to Siddhartha's aunt and foster mother, he allowed nuns into the sangha. These accounts show that women were very interested in Buddha and the Middle Way and how they taught about renouncing desire, nonviolence, and giving. Some of the women who came to the sangha shared their feelings by writing poetry. These poems that they wrote are some of the oldest recorded words that have been written by women in all of our written history.

. . .

There was one of the nuns, whose name is Sumangalamata, celebrated her freedom from living her life as a wife and free of all of the limits that a regular existence created through writing. She once wrote:

"A woman well set free! How free I am, how wonderfully free, from kitchen drudgery. Free from the harsh grip of hunger and the empty cooking pots, free, too, of that evil man, the weaver of sunshades. Calm now, and serene I am, all lust and hatred purged. To the shade of spreading trees, I go and contemplate my happiness."

In many places that follow Buddhism today, women aren't allowed to go into the sangha. However, in India and other places in the world, men and women live their lives as lay Buddhists, and they use dharma as often as they can.

Because Buddhism will accept anyone who adopts the Middle Way, it has spread quickly through various classes of people in India. Buddha and other teachers created the appropriate teachings and presented them as a message from Buddha to their audiences so they could appreciate them more.

MONASTERIES

His wandering followers soon settled down into monasteries that were given by the married clergy. These clergies were then taught some of Buddha's teachings. They also visited Buddha's birthplace and worshipped the tree, where he became enlightened. They

BUDDHISM

visited his images in temples and saw his body's relics that were housed in funeral mounds. King Ashoka and his son help spread Buddhism into Sri Lanka and South India.

His followers created most of the monastic schools. This is mainly because his teaching was a bit puzzling on many points. For example, he wouldn't give an indisputable answer about whether or not humans have souls. There were many schools because he wouldn't appoint a successor to be the sangha leader. He told his monks to be lights unto themselves and use the dharma as their guide.

Around the first century CE, a huge split happened with the Hinayana and Mahayana branches. The Ravada Schools are the only schools that remain in the Hinayana branch. They are located in Sri Lanka and throughout the Southeast Asian countries. These schools stress the historical figure of Buddha, along with practicing meditation and a monk's lifestyle. The monks within the Ravada hold onto Buddhist teachings that humans didn't have any souls when he taught about the volition, consciousness, feelings, sensations, and perceptions of the human body. They believe that humans have to be reformed and then reborn. They had to accept karma throughout their lives until they finally reached Nirvana. The Ravada School has created a sacred law of Buddha's early regulations and teachings that they call the Tripitaka.

Mahayana Schools started around the first century CE. They can still be found today in Tibet, Japan, China, and Korea. The most prominent schools are Tantra, Chanor

Zen, and Pure Land. These schools used texts called sutras. They teach that normal people can be good Buddhists, too. They also believe that other paths lead to Nirvana other than meditation, like good works and chanting. They believe that all humans and Buddha have an origin in what has been called Emptiness, Buddha Mind, and Buddha Nature. It isn't "nothing," but is more of an indescribable "Source of all Existence." It also has the potential to be Enlightenment. The historical Buddha was just one manifestation of "Buddha Nature." The Mahayana talks about many past and future Buddhas. People who have reached a "god-like" presence rule over heavenly paradises or Buddha worlds. Bodhi Sattvas are also important because they are people who have reached enlightenment but take a vow to use their power, wisdom, and compassion to help others get away from their sufferings. The Mahayana law states that there isn't a distinction between "other" and "self" or between Nirvana and Samsara or rebirth. Due to this, Bodhi Sattva can take other people's sufferings and transfer their own merits onto them.

Even though Buddhism was almost extinct in India by the 12th century CE, probably due to Muslim invasions, Hinduism's all-embracing nature, or because it was too much stress on the monks, Buddhism as a religion has proved it has vitality and spirituality in Asian countries where it has been carried. There have been many practices and forms of Buddhism that have been created that have allowed all kinds of people to satisfy their spiritual needs with this wonderful religion.

TEACHING AS JATAKAS

In order to convey Buddhism to the uneducated people, the Buddhist teachers would make up folktales. There were times

BUDDHISM

when these teachers would use the folktales as the base for retelling Buddha's previous lives before he was born as Prince Siddhartha. In the largest collection written, around 537 jatakas, they discuss his past lives in poetry but were discussed in length. Some Buddhists believe that the jatakas are true stories of his early life taken from epic perspectives. It can easily be understood how they originated from folktales. In some of them, Buddha was conceptualized as being born as a Brahmin, a Kshatriya, a peasant, and animals like rabbits or elephants. None of these have him portrayed as female, and this shows why Buddhists favor males over females.

In one jataka, the Buddha was born as Prince Five Weapons, who was a Royal Brahmin. When he encountered an ogre, he used poisoned arrows, a mighty mace, a piercing spear, and a sharp sword. All of these fail to get through the ogre's matted, sticky, and thick hair. Prince Five Weapons decided to use his forehead, feet, and fists against the ogre. This doesn't help either, and he just gets stuck to the ogre. The ogre gets ready to eat the Prince. This didn't upset the Prince; he just started telling the ogre about the Buddhist lessons that death was inevitable, fearing it was futile, and the virtue of not killing anyone. The Prince convinced the ogre of his moral and spiritual powers. The ogre releases the Prince and becomes a supporter. This is a story that teaches you not to rely on all of your senses but, instead, relies on the truth of Buddhism to overcome any foes you may have.

This story, about being connected with foes but getting away from them by using words that persuade your enemy to turn you lose, is the only version that Buddha is in. All the other stories that have been spread over the entire world for hundreds of years come from India. Even before this version, the folktale describes the way hunters trap monkeys by putting sticky things on the tree branches so they can't jump away. Over 1000 years later, an American version appears in a collection written by Uncle Remus where he wrote about Brer Rabbit getting stuck on the Tar Baby. During the story, we come to learn that Brer Rabbit succeeds in talking his way out of getting tossed into the briar patch and gets away.

Over 500 jatakas show how all the Buddhist teachers have connected with others using the common people's stories and language to tell them about Buddha's lessons in a very efficient but simple way. Within Buddhism, their social model ranks people according to their dana or donations. Nuns and monks have to give up everything and live the rest of their lives following dharma, and this puts them at the highest level of Buddhism. Common people can also follow the Middle Way; however, they are capable of. As times changed, those who could give the most, including donations to their shrines and monasteries, were always the most important people, especially those who could not give as much. This is why the rich kings and merchants who could give generously would stand that highest among the common people. People who didn't give anything to Buddhism get placed in the lowest ranks. These include Kshatriyas, Brahmins, Jains, and several other people who were part of various Varnas.

THE MIDDLE WAY TEACHINGS

Any person who follows the Middle Way and have abstained from violence and who donated could rise up by their own accounts. This is what has attracted many people to make the conversion within ancient India. The merchants who could afford to give lots of money to Buddhism and were willing to live without killing anything found this religion to be a very attractive one. To help them work through their concerns, the Buddhist scholars put together guides and lessons that showed them how to preserve their money by not giving in to their desires and ways they could prevent their children from squandering their resources.

Women and men who were part of different groups within Indian society, who didn't think that Brahmanic Varna to be all that persuasive, especially those who had a place in this model that was very low, would end up supporting and joining Buddhism. Non-Kshatriyas and Shudras, who fought their way to being kings, preferred to support Buddhism more and Brahmins less.

Many metaphysical schools were created within Buddhism. Their central concept about existing with nature went along with the Buddhist teachings. They agreed that people are incarnated many times in many different births, as either another human or an animal. These selves consisted of desires and sensory perceptions that hold onto Karma. Karma is the bad and good actions that a person has done in all their lives. As a person gives up their desires, they become unattached to their senses, and their karma gets released. Final freedom comes when every desire and attachment has been released, and they reach Nirvana. They never have to suffer through another birth, death, rebirth, or re-death anymore.

BUDDHA REACHES NIRVANA

When Buddha finally died here on earth, his body was cremated. In spite of all the Buddha's teachings about the worthlessness and unreality of our physical bodies, his followers did preserve his remains, charred bones, and teeth. For some of his followers, his remains contained the Buddha's sacred power. They wanted places to store these relics, so rich merchants and kings built stupas to house them. Every hemispheric stupa had a relic in its center. The stupa had an umbrella above it to show it was royal. And this signified Buddha's sovereignty. People would travel long distances to walk around the stupas in the clockwise direction to show homage to Buddha. This pattern slowly became the custom for some Brahmanic temples. With time, some Buddhism practices became similar to other religious traditions. This was very true for people who hadn't learned about all the metaphysics of every religion.

While many nuns and monks conformed to the ideals of not being attached to possessions, with time, some monasteries became wealthy due to wealthy donors. Some rich donors gained some clout when they gave silver, jewels, gold, and land, among other valuable things. Some monasteries were turned into learning centers, with libraries that continued to grow with time. Monks would teach their students and would develop philosophical and scholarly traditions.

ART THAT REPRESENTS BUDDHA

To visually convey Buddha's teachings, artists have used many different things to show these. Because Buddha had reached Nirvana, some earlier artists showed him in his absence. Jain artists also used this for their transcendent leaders. The earliest sculptors would create a piece of the Tree of Enlightenment, but they would not place Buddha under it, so the show is absent. By doing this, all eyes will focus on where Buddha used to be. Different sculptors show this same message by representing Buddha's footprints indented with his special markings. Others chose to use the dharma wheel that they believe rolls through the universe and establish Buddhists' law.

There are artists who came about later on the show Buddha in his human form. The Ajanta Caves in Western India have some of the best ancient Indian art. There are about 30 cave monuments cut into rocks that date to about the second century BC up to the seventh century CE. These cave walls are covered with Buddha paintings, his life events, and how he perceived the world around him.

In some of these images of Buddha, he is sometimes wearing a halo. His earlobes will be stretched to show where he would wear his golden earrings during the affluent years of his youth before he chose to abandon his palace life. They would style his hair into tight curls that had the appearance of snails. Like anything else that is sacred, Buddha is often shown to have something coming out of the top part of his head. Many art historians have explained this in various ways that range from it being a knot tied in his hair to his brain extending out of his head. There are some Jains, like Mahavira, who show Siddhartha as the ultimate self-disciplinarian. Still, this was just a very unproductive phase of life for Siddhartha that he gave up to follow the Middle Way.

THE SPREAD OF BUDDHISM

Over hundreds of years, Buddhism has become a religion all over the world. It started out by spreading through most of Asia. This began about the third century BCE when Indian missionaries traveled to Sri Lanka. This is the time when most of the population was converted. They would follow Buddha's first teachings that they referred to as the Hinayana or Theravada, which means "Lesser Vehicle." This type of Buddhism spread from Sri Lanka into Southeast Asia, and this is where it would stay dominant in Indonesia, Cambodia, Laos, Thailand, and Burma, which is now Myanmar. Other religions from India, such as Hinduism, were also present in these areas. Still, in every situation, the people living in the society would quickly adapt their religious views to work with their own cultures.

As the Buddhist ideas in India developed, the Mahayana appeared around the first century CE. This spread throughout the land into what we now know as Afghanistan. In 2001, the Taliban blew up some of the most popular statues of Buddha in Bamiyan. It was those statues that were the most extensive evidence of Buddhism that they had. When Buddhism made its way into Afghanistan, it got mixed together with the Greek culture. From Afghanistan, Buddhism made its way into China, on to Japan, and all adapted their local cultures as it moved.

The newest form of Buddhism that was developed in India became known as Vajrayana, or "Thunderbolt Vehicle" because it talks about sudden enlightenment. By the time the seventh century rolled around, this type had spread into Tibet and Nepal.

. . .

Even though India was the area in which Siddhartha taught and lived. Buddhism died out with time. This happened because Buddhism caught emperors and kings' attention, especially ones who weren't born Kshatriya. The rich merchants, along with the emperors and kings, gained a lot of notability by making huge donations to the sanghas, monasteries, and nunneries. Some became seats of great learning, but they slowly lost their connection to the common people.

Now there are about eight million Buddhists still in India. They usually go by neo-Buddhist Dalits now. The people who follow these teachings make up less than one percent of the people in India. They used India's courts to help reclaim, from the Brahmins, some of the most sacred sites for Buddha, including those in Bodh Gaya, where Buddha reached his state of enlightenment.

BUDDHIST TEACHINGS AND PRINCIPLES

WHILE THERE ARE many offshoots of Buddhism, the early Buddhist faith's basic doctrines remain the same. These basic teachings include the eight-fold path and their four noble truths. Buddhism will often describe reality in terms of a process and relation instead of entity or substance.

The experience a person has is looked at through the five aggregates. The first aggregate is formed. This is all about a person's material existence. The next four, sensations, perceptions, psychic constructions, and consciousness, refers to the psychological processes. The main idea of the Buddhist teaching of non-self explains that there aren't any independent, immutable soul or self in the five aggregates. Any phenomena come from interrelation and dependently from conditions and causes, which means they are subject to cessation and decay. These causal conditions are explained through a 12-membered chain known as the dependent origination, whose links are: ignorance, predisposition, consciousness, name-form, the senses, contact, craving, grasping, becoming, birth, old age, and death.

Since they have a very distinct view on the idea of cause and effect, Buddhism accepts the samsara belief that comes from pan-India. This explains why all living things get trapped inside a cycle of birth, death, and rebirth. Their momentum into their next rebirth comes from the mental and physical actions that they had in their previous lives. Getting released from this cycle of being reborn is transcending into what they refer to as nirvana.

For the start, meditation and moral precepts create the basis of these Buddhist practices. The five basic moral precepts that they undertake are to refrain from taking life, drinking intoxicants, speaking falsely, acting unchastely, and stealing. These are followed by the members of monastic orders and the laity. The members also have to follow five more precepts that include refraining from eating at the wrong times, watching secular entertainment, using garlands, perfumes, and other bodily adornments, sleeping in wide and high beds, and from receiving money. The monastic members are further regulated by several other rules that are called Partimoksa. The monastic order is seen as one of the three jewels, along with religious teaching and the Buddha. The practice of worshiping stupas, or the burial mounds, predated Buddhism and helped create their later ritualistic and devotional practices.

THE THREE UNIVERSAL TRUTHS

"One day, Buddha rested under the shade of a tree and saw all of the beauty of the countryside. The flowers were blooming, and the trees were creating bright new leaves, but he also noticed a lot of unhappiness through all of that beauty. A bird pecked at a worm. Then an eagle swooped down and grabbed up the bird. Troubled by what he said, he asked, 'Why must one creature eat another to survive?'"

During his process of enlightenment, he was able to uncover the answer to that question. This is when he found the three great truths of the universe. He then took what he had learned and shared it with others in a simple way to ensure everybody could understand what he was teaching.

One: "Nothing Is Lost in the Universe."

His first truth explained that nothing within the Universe is lost. Everything will transform into some type of energy, and then energy will change back into matter. A dead leaf is going to become soil. A seed will turn into a sprout and then into a new plant. Within the solar system, older systems and starts will disintegrate and create cosmic rays. All you have to do is look at yourself to see things. You were born from your parents, and then any child you have was born of you. Everything in the universe is all the same. We are the same as trees, plants, and any other human begins on the planet. We are the rain that falls. We are made up of the same things as everything around us. Everything is one and the same. If we end up destroying something, then that means we are also destroying a part of ourselves. If we end up cheating at something, then we are also cheating ourselves. After Buddha and all of his followers understood this concept, they didn't kill another animal.

Two: "Everything Changes"

The second universal truth is that all of life is changing at all times. Life is like a river that flows forever. Sometimes it will flow slowly, and other times it will flow swiftly. It will flow along gently and smoothly in some areas, but it will later rock and even pull plants up out of the ground. When we believe that nothing could possibly harm us, something unexpected will happen. Once saber-toothed tigers, dinosaurs, and mammoths roamed the land. They all died out, yet this didn't bring life to an end. Other life forms, such as smaller mammals, came into being, and then humans eventually would. We now have the ability to see the earth from space and have learned about the various changes that happen throughout the planet. Our ideas concerning life have also made major changes. People used to believe that the earth was flat and was the center of the universe, but we now know that's not true. The earth is round and rotates around the sun.

Three: "The Law of Cause and Effect"

The third truth explains that there is a continuous change because of the law of cause and effect. This cause and effect law is even discussed in our modern science books. This is one way where Buddhism and science are similar. This particular law of Buddhism is most commonly referred to as karma. Nothing happens to a person unless they deserve it. We will experience the things that we earn, and it doesn't matter if it is bad or good. The way you currently are is caused by the things you have previously done. Your actions and thoughts will determine what kind of life you are going to experience. If you make sure that you do good things, eventually, you will get that back with something just as good. If you are always doing bad things, then you will likely have something bad happen to you in the future. We are forming new karma through the things we think, do, and say every moment of our lives. If we have a good understanding of this, we don't have to fear karma. We can easily make karma our friend. It can enable us to have an amazing future.

THE TRIPLE JEWEL

Buddha knew that it was going to be quite difficult for people to follow his teachings all on their own, so he created what was known as the three refuges that they could follow. If a person intends to become Buddhist, they should rely on and take refuge in the Buddha, Sangha, and Dharma. This is what has also been called the triple jewel. The Sangha is basically the nuns and monks. These people will live within the Buddhist monasteries, and they are there to carry out Buddha's teachings. Sangha translates to a "harmonious community." These three things all possess precious qualities, just like a jewel, and they can help a person reach enlightenment.

Refuge is an area where a person can live when they need protection and safety, much like you would find shelter during a storm. When it comes to taking refuge, it isn't saying that you are trying to run away from life. It means that you are attempting to live a life that is fuller and truer. Taking refuge is just like a person who is getting ready to travel into a city that he does not know. He will need a guide that will help guide him along the path and need some traveling companions to help him.

- Buddha is your guide.
- Dharma is the path you take.
- The sanghas are the companions or teachers that you have along the way.

A person has to go through a special ceremony when they take refuge with the triple jewel. You have to recite this verse while in the presence of an ordained nun or monk with a sincere mind.

"I go to the Buddha for refuge. I go to the Dharma for refuge. I go to the Sangha for refuge."

For Buddhists, this act of taking refuge is the first thing they have to do when they start along their path of enlightenment. Even if they aren't able to reach enlightenment during this current life, they will have a better chance to find enlightenment during the next life. These people who take on the precepts is referred to as the layperson.

DHARMA

The word dharma is the most important and most used word in Buddhism. It is one of the three jewels where Buddhists can take refuge. Dharma has always been pre-eminent. It is dharma that gives the pretext for the community, and when one realizes dharma, they can become a Buddha and then binds it all together.

What exactly does dharma mean? This is a fascinating term since it integrates and includes many experience levels, from the first time you step on the path that will take you to enlightenment.

Eternal Dharma

Buddha Shakyamuni said that dharma will always be present in some of the earlier texts, and it doesn't matter if Buddha is there to teach it or sangha is there to practice it. For this dharma, it is a substratum of reality in our world and lives. It is the primordial and ultimate fact of what and who we are.

It is the main goal of every Buddhist to find their "true nature." We aren't supposed just to get a glimpse of it, but we have to identify it, rest in it, and forget all other "selves" that we might have thought we had. When we realize this, we can see that what we are doesn't have a beginning or an end. I can express itself as universal love.

So, is this eternal dharma accessible to ordinary people? No, it isn't. The truth is that it is always at the front of our consciousness, and it doesn't matter if we identify as Buddhists or not. It also doesn't matter if we have any interest in spirituality.

. . .

BUDDHISM

Dharma as Phenomena

Th. Stcherbatsky, a Buddhist scholar, wrote a book called *The Central Conception of Buddhism and the Meaning of the Word Dharma*. In this book, he informs us that dharma is the base of our existence, of our occurrences, perceptions, and thoughts that make up who we are as humans.

But, we need to have a distinction made between what we conceive to be a reality, our wishful thinking, and our preconceptions, along with its implacable, raw facts. Dharma is the extra sense that we feel in our lives, and it doesn't care if we like it or we don't, and it also doesn't matter whether we wished for it or didn't or whether we expected it or didn't. An unexpected death, the loss of a relationship, and a sudden illness are all dharma expressions. If you had ever had a light not turn on when you flipped the switch, a phone call you weren't expecting, or the joy of seeing your new grandbaby, you have felt dharma.

All of these events will just not do because they show us just how much we have been locked away in a dream that we have made. A dream of what the world is like and who we are. It can wake us up for just a minute. All this happens when it can be viewed by its own light and from its side. It proclaims the untruths of how we view the world and ourselves. Dharma, as a phenomenon, is not any different from eternal dharma. The starkness and nakedness of this phenomena show that the eternal dharma is in our lives.

. . .

Dharma As the Path

The way we respond to the destabilization and disruption that eternal dharma causes when it shows up in our lives as choices.

We might fall into denial and start looking to reinstate our security, comfort, and solidity. We could also see the dharma as a sign of our ultimate reality and then follow it as a path. Our first attempt might lead us to deny all the things we have seen and then pretend we didn't. This could cause more bondage, suffering, negative karma, and increased confusion. The next one leads us to remember the Theravadin's words and not get rid of our suffering but a gradual dissolution of anyone who suffers.

At first, the path might be painful and hard, but by meditating and following some of the other disciplines of Buddhism, we can train ourselves by going back time and time again to the edge of dharma, to the groundlessness of the moment. With some time, you will find a way to return back to relief and peace. From this point on, the path of dharma starts to unroll easily under our feet.

Teachings of Dharma

Dharma is the lesson that was given by the Buddha, and that was added to by many generations of enlightened and accomplished women and men. This dharma can evoke, point to, and describe eternal dharma as it happens in our uninterrupted and unadorned life.

. . .

Originally the teachings of dharma were all the words that were sung and spoken by an enlightened one. Buddha's words always start with: "Thus have I heard" and not "Thus have I read." Just like someone who wants to become a prima ballerina can't just read books about ballet; you have to get all the lessons from a learned teacher. In order to learn about dharma, we have to hear all we can talk about it. We have to experience the flights and eloquence of the people who have received Buddha's realization and understanding.

THE EIGHTFOLD PATH

This path is normally referred to as steps on the path and not the path itself. It was never meant to be a sequential process, but as aspects of our lives, and they need to be integrated into our lives daily. So we are creating an environment that will help us move closer to Buddha.

This path can be found in the center of the middle way that turns us away from our extremes and helps us find a simple path.

If you are the least bit religious, you are probably aware of your religion's moral codes. Muslims, Jews, and Christians all have them. Even though there is a degree of similarity across these groups, how a person interprets the codes will differ. When you look at the Ten Commandments, you will get a feeling of authority that these have to be fulfilled.

. . .

For Buddhists, the eightfold path is just meant to be a guideline, the be thought about, and then taken on when every step has been completely accepted as a part of your life. Buddhism will never ask for blind faith; it wants you to find yourself and to help you learn.

The meaning of the word right has many aspects, and it includes a balanced, ethical, or middle way. If things go right for you, you will experience unique feelings inside that will confirm all of these things as being the right action or decision.

Right Understanding or View

This is a very important step on your path because it relates to looking at the world and everything as it truly is and not the way we think it should be or we want it to be. Just like you read directions on a map, and then decide to take a trip by studying, reading, and looking at all the information you have is important if you don't want to get lost. On a deeper level, your direct experience will lead you to the Right View or Understanding. Basically, you have to have a real understanding of the way suffering and reality are interwoven. Just knowing your reality isn't of any value if you don't use it in your personal life.

Right Intent or Resolve

The next step is Right Resolve or Intent. This is when you become totally committed to the path. This step urges you to decide what we really want. This step has to come from our hearts and involves seeing the equality of every life and having compassion for every life, and this has to start with you. You have to have a passion and persistence for this journey. If you decide you want to climb Mount Everest, you have to understand all its pitfalls and the lay of the land. You have to know all the equipment you are going to need and who you need to take with you. You will only be able to climb that mountain if you want to and are passionate about climbing it. Basically, you need to have a desire to act with the right intentions without doing any harm.

Right Speech

The next step is Right Speech. Most people tend to underestimate how powerful words can be. We usually regret what comes out of our mouths after we speak. Everybody has experienced a disappointment that came from harsh criticism, whether or not it was justified. You have to recognize all truths and be aware of the impact that idle gossip and repeating rumors can have. Thoughtfully communicating with others can unite you with others and can heal all disagreements. When you resolve not to ever speak in anger or unkindly to anyone, you will create a spirit of consideration that will move you closer to living a compassionate life. Basically, you have to stop lying. You also can't use abusive or divisive language.

Right Action

This step recognizes that there is a need to take an ethical approach to life. You have to think about others and the world. This means that we can't take things that aren't given to us, and we have to respect any agreement that you make in your business and private lives. This encircles the five precepts that were given to us by Buddha that say you can't kill, lie, have sexual misconduct, and don't partake of any intoxicants. This step means we have to not just think about humans but the environment in general. We have to keep the world safe for other generations. Basically, you have to act in ways that won't do any harm to anyone or anything like not killing, not stealing, and abstaining from any kind of sexual misconduct.

Right Livelihood

If you don't respect life, then this becomes a barrier between you and the path. Buddhism promotes equality for every being and respects every life. Specific kinds of works were discouraged by Buddha, especially if you are dealing with intoxicants and drugs that could harm you. It also discourages you from dealing with weapons and harming humans or animals. Buddha would never tell you to open a liquor store or work in one. You couldn't have a butcher shop or a gun shop. He also discourages trading human lives or having slaves. He also didn't like fortune tellers as they made assumptions about a person's future. This implies that if you can do some work either as a part of your community, in an actual job, or do some community or home-based service. Most monks make sure that every member will have a chore they have to do each day that will remind them to take this step on their path. Basically, you have to make a good living while being completely honest in all business decisions.

Right Effort

This step says you have to be enthusiastic while having a positive attitude. Just like the strings on a musical instrument, how much effort you put into it shouldn't be too impatient or tense. It also can't be too laid back or slack. The right effort needs to produce an attitude of cheerful and steady determination. If you want to move on with this step, you have to have honest and clear thoughts that come easy while anger and jealousy get left behind. This is equal to positive thinking that gets followed by focused action. Buddha was way ahead of the time with this one because many books have been written about how powerful having the right attitude can be.

Right Mindfulness

Even though Right Effort is a fairly easy concept for many people, this one is a bit tricky and might involve the way you think. Having the right mindfulness means you need to be aware of every moment. You need to be focused on every moment. If you are traveling, hear a noise, see buildings, trees, billboards, feel movements, think about people you have lost, or think about where you are going, you live in the moment. This step asks us to be aware of every moment on our journey. We need to have an undistracted and clear mindset at every moment. This is close to meditation. You need to understand that you aren't trying to exclude the world, but it is just the opposite. This step asks us to be aware of every moment and the actions we are taking in these moments. When you are aware, you will be able to see how your old habits and patterns control you. By being aware, you might see how fear of failure limits our actions. There might be times when you become absorbed in what you are doing. It might be a sport, art, or music. Have you done anything when your mind is only on that activity? If so, you were mindful in that moment. Basically, you have to be mindful of your mental qualities, mind, feelings, and body.

Right Concentration

When you have your mind uncluttered, you will be able to concentrate better so you can achieve your goals. For this step, we have to focus on one object completely. It might be a concept, a candle flame, or a flower. This can help form the next part of meditation. This step implies that we have to select something worthy to concentrate on. Once you get to a deeper level, you might not need an object to concentrate on. This step's benefits are significant because they teach your mind to see things as they truly are and not as we have been conditioned to see them. These things can lead you to feel peaceful and calm with the world. When you are in the moment and can efficiently concentrate, you will have a sense of joy. You will be able to release yourself from all the past pains, and your future mind will bring you closer to having freedom from your suffering. Basically, you need to practice skillful meditation and be informed of all the above aspects.

WHEEL OF LIFE

There are many different levels that the wheel of life can be interpreted. The drawing of the wheel of life represents the rebirth cycle. There are six main sections on the wheel, and these represent the six realms. You can look at these as states of mind, or forms of existence, into which a person can be born based on their previous karma. You could also choose to look at these various realms as different personality types or different situations in life.

In each realm, the Bodhisattva Avalokiteshvara looks to show how to become liberated from this cycle of life, death, and rebirth. Liberation can only be possible in the human realm. From that point, those who find enlightenment can find a way out of the Wheel of Nirvana. This is one of the most talked-about pieces of Buddhist art.

Most Buddhists see the Wheel as an allegory and not something literal. As you look over the different areas of the wheel, you may notice that you relate to certain sections or recognize people you might know.

The outer circle is the "Paticca Samuppada," or the links of Dependent Origination. In most versions of the wheel, this is seen as a blind woman or man that represents ignorance. Then there is a potter who represents formation. A monkey is meant to represent consciousness. There will be two men in a boat that shows body and mind. There should be a house with six windows to show the senses. A couple that is hugging each other to represent contact. An eye that is being pierced by an arrow represents sensation. A person who is drinking represents thirst. A man who is gathering fruit to represent grasping. A couple who is making love that represents becoming. A woman who is giving birth that represents birth. Lastly, there is a man carrying a corpse that represents death.

There is a creature that holds the Wheel of Life. This is Yama, the Lord of the Hell Realm. Yama is representative of impermanence, and he looks at you over the top of the wheel. Despite how he looks, Yama is not believed to be an evil being. He is simply wrathful and wants to make sure that he protects Buddhism and its followers. While many are frightened by the concept of death, it isn't actually evil, only inevitable.

The first realm is the realm of the gods, Devas, and is the highest realm. It is always located at the top of the Wheel. While this area may sound like it is a nice place, it isn't perfect. Those who have been born in this space will live a life filled with pleasure. They have power, happiness, and wealth, so what could be wrong with this realm?

Since the Devas are living such happy and rich lives, they don't fully understand what suffering is. This means that their happiness is a complete curse because they won't have the motivation to get out of their cycle of birth and rebirth. They will have an end to their happy life, and they may end up being born into a realm that isn't as happy.

The Devas are in a constant battle with the second realm, the Realm of Asuras. These are jealous gods and are filled with paranoia. The people in this realm are extremely paranoid, and they are extremely competitive. They always want to beat out any competition they may have. Their first priority, though, is to reach the top. Asuras believe they belong to the God Realm and try to fight their way in.

Then the third realm moves us into the area of Hungry Ghosts. In this realm, all of the people are extremely hungry, but they think necks prevent nourishment from passing through. Food will turn to ash and fire in their mouth. That means they are always hungry. Jealousy and greed are what will cause you to be born into this realm.

The fourth realm is the Hell Realm. Terror, anger, and claustrophobia mark this realm. It is depicted as part of the ice and part fire. Within the fiery area, there are Narakas, or Hell Beings, who face torment and pain. Then in the icy area, the people are just frozen. They are abusive and angry and drive away anybody who could befriend them. Icy hell-beings push people away by being unfeeling and cold. In their isolation, they turn their aggression inwards and become self-destructive.

The fifth realm is the animal realm. The Tiryakas are predictable, solid, and regular. They cling to the things that are familiar and even fear things that they don't know. It is marked by complacency and ignorance. During their life, they are always looking for comfort, and they avoid anything that causes discomfort. There is no humor within their life. While they can feel contentment, they will also just as easily become fearful if they find themselves in a new situation.

The sixth realm is the human realm. This is where liberation from the Wheel becomes possible. This realm is filled with curiosity and questioning. This is the space of human beings and passion. Dharma is openly available in this realm, but there are just a few who will seek it out. The remainder of people will end up getting caught within the cycle of acquiring, consuming, and striving.

In the middle of the wheel live the forces that keep it moving. These three things are greed, ignorance, and anger. To represent these, you will find a pig, snake, and rooster depicted. Anger, ignorance, and greed are considered the "Three Poisons" this is because they poison the person who harbors them. This is what forces life to continue moving.

SCHOOLS OF BUDDHISM

In the centuries after Buddha lived, his disciplines continued to spread his teachings through Asian countries. Over the years, Buddhism has been split into two many schools: Mahayana and Theravada. The definition of Theravada is "the teachings of the Elders." The monks within this school follow the same practices that were started by Buddha and passed down through the years, such as meditating and living in the forests. The goal within this school is for them to become an Arhat, which is basically a person that does not suffer. This is most commonly found within southern Asian countries, like Myanmar, Thailand, and Sri Lanka.

Mahayana stresses the act of going out and doing good in the world. Mahayana translates to "Great Vehicle." The main goal of this is to be on the Bodhisattva Path. Bodhisattva refers to people who enlighten themselves and others. It is mainly found in northern Asian countries like Japan, Vietnam, Korea, Tibet, and China.

Buddha, himself, never wrote anything down. His followers did. They collected these into books known as Sutras. There are many Sutras, so there is no one holy book. The first of the Sutras were written in Sanskrit and Pali on palm leaves. They were gathered into a collection known as the Tripitaka, meaning "three baskets." This breaks down into three sections:

1. "Sutra Pitaka – Sutras and the explanation."
2. "Vinaya Pitaka – Rules for nuns and monks."

3. "Abhidharma Pitaka – The philosophy and psychology of Buddha's teachings."

They always treat sutras with respect and place them in the most respected space.

You'll also find a lot of symbols in Buddhist teachings. This has led people to believe that Buddhists worship idols. This isn't true. They actually do bow and make incense and flower offerings in honor of the Buddha, not to some image or idol of him. During this, they take the time to meditate on the virtues of Buddha. They also have different Bodhisattva and Buddha images that depict various qualities. For example, there is a Buddha who has hands that are resting in his lap, and this is to help remind you to develop peace within. Traditional offerings given to Buddha include:

- Food – reminds us to give out the best
- Water – represents purity
- Incense – reminds one to be peaceful
- Light from candles or lamps – symbolizes wisdom
- Flowers – a reminder of how fast things change

Within their mediations and ceremonies, they use what is known as Dharma instruments. Each of these instruments has a certain use.

- Wooden fish – keeps the rhythm

- Gongs – announces activities and ceremonies
- Drums – keeps the rhythm and announces ceremonies
- Bells – gives signals in mediations and ceremonies

The lotus flower is also important to Buddhists. It represents enlightenment because it grows in the mud. Also representative of enlightenment is the Bodhi tree. It is a type of fig tree and has been named the tree of enlightenment.

BUDDHIST FESTIVALS

The Buddhists hold many festivals during the year. They are meant to celebrate various important happenings that occurred during the life of Buddha and important teachers and Bodhisattvas. During celebrations, people will have the chance to take refuge and precepts or decide to become a nun or monk.

Buddha Day

This is the most important event of the year for Buddhists as it celebrates the birth of Buddha. It is always celebrated on the full-moon day in May. During this celebration, they will always have the ceremonial bathing of Buddha. During this ceremony, they will pour cups of scented water over the baby Buddha statue. This act helps to purify a person's actions and thoughts. They elaborately decorate the temples with banners and flowers. The altars are filled with offerings. The day is a joyous one for everybody.

. . .

Dharma Day

Dharma Day, or Asalha Puja, is always celebrated on the full-moon in July. This holiday is meant to commemorate the first lesson that the Buddha taught to the five monks in Deer Park. It is not as extravagant as Buddha Day, but it is still an important holiday.

Sangha Day

This celebration, also known as Kathina Day, is typically celebrated in October. They teach that the nuns and monks within Theravada went away on a three-month retreat during what would have been the rainy season. Once they returned from their retreat, the laity would offer them robes and anything else they needed. This celebration is meant to symbolize the close relationship between the laity and Sangha.

Ullambana

This holiday is all based upon the story of Maudglyayana, who was one of the disciples of Buddha. When his mother passed away, he wanted to know which realm she had been reborn into. Through the use of his spiritual gifts, he made his way into the various realms and discovered that she was suffering from an unquenching hunger. He took her food, but it would turn into hot coals whenever she would take a bite. This upset him, and he asked Buddha, "Why is my mother suffering in the hells?" To which Buddha said, "In her life as a human, she was stingy and greedy. This is her retribution." Buddha told him that he should, "Make offerings to the Sangha. The virtue and merit from this act will release your mother and others from the hells."

This resulted in Maudgalyana giving offerings, which caused his mother and thousands of other people to be released from hell—after this, giving offerings in honor of deceased loved ones so they would be released from hell became a popular practice in Mahayana countries. This holiday occurs typically sometime during September.

BUDDHISM NUMBERS

IT WON'T TAKE you long to realize that there are many numbers in Buddhism. You will find four of this, seven of that, and eight of something else. Their numeral sequence organizes some of the main scriptures, like the Ekottara. This brings up a question: what do all of these numbers mean? Are they just a way to organize information, or is there something else to it?

Let's begin with some general observations. Buddhism started as a religion during the Axial Age. This was a time that was characterized by moving away from the old, symbolic, and mythic ways of thought to the more linear, rational thoughts. During the Axial Age, all the religions had philosophies and a character with two faces called "Janus's face." The face in front looked for compassion and reason. The face in the back looked back to the age of myth and magic. It is because they use reasoning that it appeals to our modern consciousness and because they preserve the symbolism that they appeal to our subconscious.

. . .

This "conscious" relates to numbers as rationality, which is the definition of perfect, abstract logic. But the "unconscious" takes more of an interest in numerology or the hidden meanings of numbers. This kind of thing would never be put into the Academe, except as something to be curious about. Today it has more followers than proper mathematics.

With all of our modern bias, we can see numbers being used in many Buddhist texts, and our first assumption is to just look at them as a way to count without any meaning behind them. It will soon be obvious that most numbers just can't be taken literally. You might know that 500 actually stands for hundreds. There are other cases where numbers are given, like literal measurements when they are relating to Mount Meru or mythical sea creatures. You can see that there are some uses of numbers that don't make any sense whatsoever.

How far back does this go? If a sea creature's size can't be taken as literal, what should we do with all those huge numbers given to the life spans during various realms? Some of the details can't be so easily falsified. What about the number seven is found in various texts, or as we like to say, "the seven lines of a stream" is also symbolic.

The modern system of numbers comes from two sources. One is the basic counting system based on the number ten derived from practicing counting by using your fingers. Children are still being taught to do it this way. Our fingers are the basis where the metaphor of numbers was created.

. . .

It was a big leap to take out "one apple equals one finger" and just have numbers. Even adults need some type of physical aid to help us with things that go beyond basic mathematics. The base system often is more practical. It can deal with "the here and now." It could be used in construction where building sizes get measured by using body parts or in trades where an easy way of weighing or counting might be needed. Sumer's most ancient writing consisted mostly of bills of trade, which had endless lists of grain, goats, and camels being sold and transported from one place to another.

Another source that is more famous in the sky. All the months in a year, which is usually 12, relates to the year's approximate days, which is around 365. Astronomical number systems are based on 12 or, in Sumer's case, 60. We have done away with the 60 system for everything except the way we measure time. Clocks still rotate in cycles of 60 and 12: 60 seconds in a minute, 60 minutes in one hour, 12 hours in the morning, and 12 hours in the evenings. This mimics the heavens while reminding us about the sciences' early inspiration and giving us our sense of wonder.

Let's look at the basic numbers used in the Buddhist texts and how they were used. These are just things that I have noticed during my studies over the years, but I haven't done any in-depth studies. These are just some random suggestions.

- Eka – One

This stands for cosmic unity. The Vedas' main number is "that one thing," that lies before all. The number one represents the spiritual union, a return, and healing from the broken world. The number one in Buddhism is the same way, except that their healing union wasn't metaphysical but actually psychological.

- Dve – Two

Just like with many numbers, the Indo-European root shows how similar this number is with Pali and English. The number two represents the body when a person falls apart. You can see this in dichotomy, diversity, and division. All the original primordial Spirits or Beings are split into two separate beings that simultaneously oppose and desire each other. Right – left, female-male, night – day: the world of oppositions and binaries come into play. The number two will always yearn for the lost half.

- Tayo – Three

The number three stands for the integration of the profane and the Divine. Most religions are full of trinities. The Christian trinity refers to the Father, the Son, and the Holy Spirit. Its basic meaning will always find a way to manifest or express the relationship between the wanted unity and the world's diversity. This can be seen in the Chinese symbol of Yin and Yang, which was found in Rome hundreds of years before China. The yin and yang duality is encased in a circle, which was the original One.

BUDDHISM

The Three Vedas represent the voice of the Divine Truth as it manifests and speaks to the world. In the Pali, it has the triad of "good, bad, and undeclared." The undeclared stands for all that don't fit within the world's duality.

- Cattaro – Four

The basis for this number comes from the four directions. So this means that the number four carries a connotation of balance, perfections, encompassing, and completion. Within this sense, "The Four Noble Truths" were similar to the elephant's footprint that can cover any other footprints. The Four Assemblies create complete, balanced, and perfect sasana. This is the most used number in Buddhist texts. Even though it is the most common by itself, it can be found in a "strengthened" form in the number eight. Eight can be broken down into four main directions and four intermediate directions. Ten can be broken down into the directions while adding in below and above. These numbers will sometimes appear in more elaborate forms or geometric sets. The most beautiful is the Dhammacakkappavattana Sutta, which includes the "12 Aspects of Penetrations to the Truths," the "Eight-Fold Path," and the "Four Noble Truths" that Buddha gave us when he reached enlightenment.

- Panca – Five

In Pali, this represents the hand. The basic division of the hand divides it into four fingers and one thumb. In the five Indriyas or five spiritual faculties, wisdom will always be at the peak held up by the other four. The four here are stillness of the mind; memory or mindfulness, perseverance, persistence, energy, belief, conviction, or faith. These can be imagined like rafters holding up a ridge pole.

- Cha – Six

I am not completely positive about the metaphysical symbolism for six. Still, it could come from the astronomical cycle, and it could be related to the description of the six senses.

- Satta- Seven

*T*his seems to be the most used number in magic, especially when dealing with death and life magic. It relates to two phenomena: the female's menstrual cycle and the lunar cycles. In these, you have a return and a cycle, but you also have death and rebirth. The moon will die every month. The sun dies each day. A woman's fertility governs over death and life. The number seven can be found throughout rituals and myths. The main idea can be seen in the Christian Bible in the Book of Genesis, where God created the world in seven days. The number seven can be seen throughout Buddhism: Buddha took seven steps after he was born; Maya's death took seven days, etc. It also carries over into Buddhist folktales, where a person's soul can cross over after seven days. Other cases aren't as clear, like "the seven lives of the stream-enterer" can be taken literally.

I won't go any farther. The other numbers are normally combinations of the basic ones. There isn't a lot written about numbers in

Buddhism, but there are some notes in the Pali Dictionary. Let's look specifically at Number Three, Number Four, and Number Five in Buddhism, as these have more specific meanings.

NUMBER THREE

The number three has been associated with many different things in Buddhism.

Three Doors of Liberation

Buddhism has three marks of existence, and they are no self, suffering, and impermanence. The three doors of liberation teach how to get rid of duality, which causes all suffering by living according to these truths. It is the good side of some very bad news.

1. Aimlessness: This means that we will constantly be running after enlightenment, happiness, wealth, love, etc. Being aimless means that you don't have any goals or anything to pursue. You will then realize that you have everything that you needed the entire time.

1. Sinlessness: Sinlessness is when we aren't attached to temporary things. This is a person's outer appearance of things or their sign, and it can be very deceiving. A cloud looks innocent, but then suddenly it begins to rain but then the rain waters all the plants. The cloud changes

forms, but nothing gets lost. Once we realize sinlessness, we rise above birth and death and will be able to enjoy our wonderful life journey.

1. No Self: Because nothing has a self that is separate because everything in the universe is connected. In order to describe this, Thich Nhat Hanh created the term "interbeing." Once we realize that we are connected to everything, we will have perfect communication with everything and live with ease and joy.

Three Aspects of Refuge

The Dharma, the Sangha, and the Buddha are known as "the Triratna" or "the Triple Jewels or Gems."

- Dharma: this refers to the commentaries, lessons, and teachings of Buddhism. The teachings' body described the Buddhist belief and doctrine.
- Sangha: this is a group of people who follow Buddha and all that he teaches. This was first interpreted to be the ordained celibate monks who only served Buddha, but modern Buddhists extend this meaning to include all the common people who follow Buddha.
- Buddha: this is talking about Buddha's Divine nature. The actual person of Siddhartha Gautama or Buddha Sakyamuni.

So every time you bow, every time you put a stick of incense into a burner, you recall one of those "Jewels" or essential elements of Buddha.

Three Prostrations

When you visit a statue of Buddha, you are supposed to bow three times before the Sangha, Dharma, and Buddha. You can also bow before "any sacred object of veneration." Bowing is seen as a way to purify the mind, speech, and body of any karmic defilement like pride. You will also offer them three incense sticks. If you walk around a tomb or temple, you have to do this three times, too.

The Three Yanas

There are three stages of the journey to enlightenment in Buddhism. These are also known as yanas. Yanas get translated into vehicles that move you along the path to enlightenment. Even though every yana creates the path that leads to the next one, there isn't a certain way you should practice them.

1. Individual Liberation

We have to begin by working on ourselves. This yana will focus on the foundational teachings like the "Four Noble Truths," the "Three Marks of Existence," plus practicing awareness and mindfulness. The end result will be the person's salvation because you will be free from the illusion of an independent and fixed self and all the suffering that it could cause yourself and others.

1. Yana of Compassion and Wisdom

We have to make sure that we deal with being attached to our personal ego, but we could still be holding onto the world. We will likely need to get rid of this by showing compassion and teaching other people about emptiness. The end result of this yana is that we have become free. We are free of both our clinging selves and other people. We will have endless compassion for everything and everyone.

1. Tantric Yana of Indestructible Wakefulness

This yana takes "the fruition as the path," since enlightenment is the beginning point along with the goal. It has also been called "the path of skillful means" since it teaches many methods to eliminate negativity and show our real nature as perfect and free. There is a large emphasis in the yana for the guru to be the teacher. Buddha enlightenment can be achieved in your lifetime by using the above methods.

The Three Sufferings

There are good reasons why Buddhists are obsessed with suffering. Suffering is the main issue that Buddhism addresses, and being able to recognize your own suffering are the first step. Suffering is considered a universal truth, along with nonself and impermanence. It is one of the three marks of existence, but it can come in many forms. In order to help you see your suffering, Buddhists broke it down into various categories.

Even though there are many subcategories, we have been asked to think about the three patterns of suffering that are in our lives.

1. All-pervasive suffering: This is the suffering that we probably don't recognize, but it will be the most instructive if we can do it. It is the background of insecurity and anxiety that clouds our happiest moments. We have a deep-set fear that life won't give us solid ground and that our existence is questionable. As Buddhists see it, these doubts are very well-founded, and when we explore them, it can give us a glimpse into wisdom.

1. The "suffering or change:" Anytime you get the things you want, you won't be able to hold onto it. Even if the things in your life are going great at this moment, it will just be a matter of time before things start going wrong. The most successful and richest people will eventually lose everything.
2. The "suffering of suffering:" This is the one that everyone is familiar with. It is the pain at birth, suffering during old age, suffering during sicknesses, and suffering in death.

The Trikaya or The Three Bodies

Buddha can manifest himself in three bodies: the Emanation Body, the Body of Bliss, and the Truth Body.

The Three Roots of Buddhism

These are the Dakini or Dharmapala, the Yidam, and the Guru.

- The Dakini or Dharmapala: this is the companion who might influence you, just like being in Shanghai with sisters and brothers in Dharma.
- The Yidam: this is the method or practice to reach a goal such as Dharma.
- The Guru: this is a person who embodies the qualities that represent both goal and aspiration. Buddha would be considered the Guru.

The Three Wise Buddhas

These are those cute little statues of the laughing Buddhas that are usually seen as three little monkeys. A proverb goes with them of being in the right action, speech, and mind.

- Buddha One: The Kikazaru has his ears covered, so he doesn't hear any evil.

- Buddha Two: The Mizaru has his eyes covered so that he doesn't see any evil.
- Buddha Three: the Iwazaru has his mouth covered so that he doesn't speak any evil.

FOUR NOBLE TRUTHS

Buddhism has been framed around these four truths. They are considered noble because they can free us from all suffering. They are the basic teachings of Buddha and encompass his whole path.

- Suffering

Our lives will always involve some sort of suffering in both subtle and obvious forms. Even though things seem to be going well, we will always feel some kind of uncertainty and anxiety inside us.

- Suffering's Cause

The main cause of our suffering is fundamental and craving ignorance. We suffer from this because we believe that we are a solid, independent, and separate entity. We are the only "I." The futile and painful struggle to keep this delusion of ego is called samsara, or cyclic existence.

- Suffering's End

There is some good news and that our sufferings are only temporary. These will be like clouds passing over the sun and obscuring from our sight temporarily. The sun in this metaphor would be the enlightened nature that is always with us. This means that our suffering will be able to end since our sufferings could be purified, and we can have an awakened mind.

- The Path

If you can live an ethical life, meditate regularly, and develop wisdom, we will be able to take the exact same journey to freedom and enlightenment from suffering that Buddha did so many years before. We have the ability to wake up, too.

THE FOUR NEGATIONS

According to Buddhism, all the concepts we have about our reality are inaccurate, incomplete, and block the way we experience how things really are. The philosophy of the Middle Way gives us reason to nullify our concepts about reality. This logic looks at four possibilities: things can be real, unreal, both, or none of them, and it will reject them. By this definition, the four negations will be:

- Not Real
- Not Unreal
- Not Both Unreal and Real
- Not Neither Unreal nor Real

We could look at reality another way: "as one," as various things that are separate, or a combination of any of these. So by this definition, the four negations will be:

- Not One
- Not Many
- Not Both Many and One
- Not Neither Many Nor One

You have the ability to practice the "Four Negations" by studying all its arguments and why any declaration about reality can become self-defeating. You could use it as a type of riddle. Accept that things aren't real, unreal, both, or neither. Think about where this will leave you. It really won't matter because the Middle Way will cut through the perception and will point you in the direction of reality's true nature.

THE FOUR FOUNDATIONS OF MINDFULNESS

The four foundations of mindfulness are Buddha's teachings about meditation. Common for all Buddhist traditions, this is a guide to help you practice mindfulness in stages.

- Being Mindful of Your Body

Being fully aware of the experience of being in your body and includes your breathing, movements within and of your body, your body's weight, posture, its impermanence, etc. This will ground you at the moment.

- Being Mindful of Feelings

Paying attention and noticing neutral, unpleasant, and pleasant feelings. This is the most elementary level of feelings. This isn't the type of "feelings" that we feel as emotions. Being mindful of your feelings will let you develop awareness without judging whatever might happen.

- Being Mindful of Your Mind

You need to be aware of your emotions and thoughts as they come up, stay around, and then go away. This lets you see any insubstantial and transient qualities of your emotional filters and thought processes that guide your actions.

- Being Mindful of Mental Objects

You need to pay attention to your entire experience while encompassing all the mental qualities and phenomena that emerge every moment. By seeing how you try to construct a world that is coherent from a series of mental events, you will understand how existence is not permanent.

THE FOURFOLD SANGHA

Sangha means community, and it is one of the three jewels in Buddhism. Normally, the sangha gets divided into four categories that are called the fourfold sangha:

- Common women
- Common men
- Nuns
- Monks

*A*re these types of practitioners important? Considering the Buddha said that he wouldn't enter Nirvana until he had followers from all the above categories who had been trained, were learned, and accomplished in dharma, then and only then would he have finished his work.

*B*uddhism hasn't always valued these sanghas equally. For hundreds of years, shangha only referred to one category, and that was monks. This has been changing in modern times. In the West and Asia, there has been a resurgence in the past several decades of fully ordinating nuns and the common women and men who are taking on bigger roles within their communities.

*T*he fourfold sangha is important because it reflects the increasing role of common people teaching about Buddha with understanding, sharing the teachings, and practicing Buddhism. The fourfold sangha won't exclude anyone while holding everyone to their highest expectations.

THE FOUR BRAHMAVIHARAS

The Brahmaviharas are four states of mind or emotions that are prized. These give us the framework to get rid of the harmful behaviors while creating positive ones. These are also known as "divine abodes" since they are states of mind where all people who have been enlightened life. They have been known as "four immeasurables" or "four limitless ones" since they represent goodwill and love toward all attentive people without limits.

The four brahmaviharas are:

- Equanimity
- Sympathetic
- Compassion
- Loving-kindness

Some teachers have described these as "the only emotions that are worth having." By cultivating these, you won't just develop boundless love, but they will undo what Buddha called their enemies: jealousy, envy, pity, and indifference.

You could bring one or more of these to mind to renew your connection to other people throughout your day. You could cultivate these through meditation. First, you need to stabilize your mind by being mindful, meditating, or calm abiding. Then you have to bring each of these into your mind, first toward yourself, and with time, toward all people.

FOUR SCHOOLS OF BUDDHISM

Since there are so many unique terms, practices, and lineages within the world of Buddhism, it could get a bit confusing. Here is a short description of the four main schools and their main practices.

- Sadkya: This is the smallest of the four schools. Its lineage was founded during the 11th century by Drogmi, who was a translator and scholar who studied Buddhism under the Indian master Naropa. Their main practice is "Lamdre or Path and Its Fruit."

- Kagyu: This school specializes in Vajrayana practices that get passed from teacher to student orally. Its lineage can be traced back to the yogi Naropa, his student Marpa, and the celebrated yogi Milarepa. Their main practices are "The Six Yogas of Naropa" and Mahamudra.

- Nyingma: This school is the original Buddhist in Tibet. They were founded by the Vajrayana master Padmasambhava who brought Buddhism into Tibet. The nine-step Nyingma path that ends at Dzogchen.

- Gelugpa: This was founded during the 15th century. This is the largest and newest school. The Dalai Lama has always been a Gelugpa, even though it isn't actually its leader. Their main practices include the Lam Rim or "Stages of the Path" and Madhyamika or "Middle Way" practices.

THE FIVE RECOLLECTIONS

Pithy and frank, these five reminders about karma and impermanence's reality can be attributed back to Buddha. Even though they begin with the bad news, thinking about the five recollections can help you accept all of the difficulties in life, and this can motivate us to practice kindness toward other people and ourselves.

1. I will grow old. There isn't any way to escape this.
2. I will have illnesses. There isn't any way to escape this.
3. I will eventually die. There isn't any way to escape this.
4. Everything and everyone that I hold near and dear to me will change. There isn't any way to escape this.
5. My closest companions are my deeds. I benefit from my deeds. The ground I stand on is my deeds.

THE FIVE BUDDHA FAMILIES

In the tantra, the Buddha family is the best way to work with and understand our emotional energies. Every family represents a certain emotion that has an enlightened and confusing aspect. These families are the embodiment of the five ancient buddhas.

1. Karma: This is the all-accomplishing wisdom. Its confusion is envy and jealousy. Karma has been associated with wind energy and summer. It has been represented by Amoghasiddhi, who resides in the north. Its color is green.
2. Padma: This is a pearl of discriminating wisdom that lets us see clearly what we need. Its confusion is possessiveness or passion. It has been associated with fire,

blossoming, and spring. It has been represented by Amitabha Buddha, who lives in the west. Its color is red.
3. Ratna: This has equanimity wisdom and is confused by pride. It has been associated with generosity, autumn, and richness. It has been represented by Ratnasambhava, who lives in the south. Its color is yellow.
4. Vajra: This has a pearl of mirror-like wisdom that reflects directly and purely. Its confusion is anger. It is associated with water and winter. It has been represented by Akshobhya, who lives in the east. Its color is blue.
5. Buddha: This has the wisdom of all-encompassing space. Its confusion is ignorance. It is associated with the open sky. It has been represented by Vairocana Buddha, who lives in the middle of the mandala. Its color is white.

THE FIVE POWERS

These powers are qualities that work in a certain order to support a person's awakening. These powers are just one of the seven quality sets that are needed for awakening. They have also been called the five strengths.

1. Faith
2. Energy
3. Mindfulness
4. Concentration
5. Wisdom

This power creates energy, which makes it possible for us to be mindful. Being mindful can lead to deeper concentration, and this finally gives way to wisdom.

These are very powerful because they control their opposites. Faith masters doubt—energy masters laziness. Mindfulness controls carelessness. Concentration masters distractions. Wisdom masters ignorance. Once you have these five powers strongly developed, our minds won't be bound by negative energies, and our compassion and understanding will flourish.

Other qualities that are needed for awakening are: "the noble eightfold path," "the seven factors of enlightenment," "the five spiritual faculties," "the four bases of supernatural power," "the four right exertions," "and the four establishments of mindfulness."

THE FIVE PRECEPTS

How could Buddhists know if they are living an ethical life? The best way is by keeping the five precepts. These are a set of guidelines for people who don't want to harm anyone or anything.

When we take refuge in "the Triple Gems," you have taken the first step in learning all about Buddhism. You have to observe the precepts by implementing those principles into daily living. Every Buddhist needs to observe these precepts once they have taken refuge in the "Triple Gem" since the precepts are the foundation of all virtuous actions and the moral standard for humans. Living by the precepts is like following your school's rules or the laws of your community. The main difference is that the school's rules and community laws are external restrictions and these precepts are a type of self-discipline. If a person is driving on an expressway and doesn't obey the traffic laws, they might get in an accident. By the same means, if someone doesn't observe all the precepts, they will break the rules and bring trouble into their life. Because of this, Buddhists have to observe all the precepts daily.

Some Buddhists will follow these literally if they can, while other people take a more situational approach. They are always guided by compassion, and whatever gives them the most benefits. There are several sets of precepts, but the most common to every Buddhist is the Five Root Precepts.

- No Killing

It is tempting to automatically think about one of the Ten Commandments here of "Thou Shalt Not Kill," but this precept has been applied to many situations.

When this precept tells you not to kill, it means that you can't harm or terminate other lives. This includes humans, insects, mice, cockroaches, or any other living thing. Since Buddhism is considered an anthropocentric religion, this is normally aimed at not killing other humans since this would be unforgivable and a major violation. Repenting won't decrease how severe the consequences will be for violating this precept. Even though killing insects is a violation, it will have less severe consequences.

Destroying a type of natural resource or wasting time is another type of killing since Buddhism teaches us that life has been accumulated with time. The earth forming substances or materials take effort and time, so if you waste time will waste shared resources, and it becomes a type of killing.

- No Stealing

*A*gain you might be thinking about the Ten Commandments, but this precept goes a lot deeper. This basically means you can't intrude on another person's wealth and property. Basically, this means that you can't take anything that doesn't belong to you without permission. This means anything that is publicly or privately owned. Robbing other people during the day is also theft. Stealing is a severe violation of an important and basic precept. Taking stationery and utensils for your personal use or borrowing anything without returning might not be a violation but is thought to be an impure act, and you will have to face the consequences of these actions. This precept might just be the hardest one to observe.

- Refrain From Sexual Misconduct

*T*his means that you can't ever have any type of sexual activity that happens outside of marriage. This means bigamy, prostitution, rape, trading humans, obstructing a person's happiness, seducing someone who isn't your marital partner, any other immoral sexual act will be a violation of this precept. If you secretly love someone but don't take any action might not violate this precept, but if your mind is thinking impure thoughts, then you aren't living a free life since the purpose of doing the precepts is to purify your mind and body.

Sexual misconduct can be a fire in the middle of an unsettled society. If a married couple doesn't commit any type of sexual misuse, they will have a harmonious and happy family, and their moral standard will be kept.

Most Buddhists today will tell you that it isn't about who you are and aren't able to have sex with but the way you relate to them. Clearly, not thinking about your partner's feelings would be a misuse of this precept along with not getting consent.

- Refrain From Wrong Speech

There might be times when you think a "little white lie" won't hurt anyone, but what good can come from gossip and deception?

No lying means you can't speak any frivolous words like harsh language, slandering, lying, and words that will stir up trouble between others. Exaggeration is a violation, but lying could be divided into lies of convenience, minor lies, and major lies.

- Lies of Convenience: This is known as "good-intentioned misrepresentation. Look at this example: your doctor

might hide the truth from you about a terminal illness to protect your emotional well being. Any lie that is told to benefit others is considered to be a lie of convenience.
- Minor Lies: This means fabricating, concealing the truth, misrepresenting, or bearing false witness are all forms of minor lies.
- Major Lies: Buddhists who have reached enlightenment or have supernatural powers but haven't done so have severely violated this precept. Another serious infringement is criticizing the Buddhist disciples' four categories, especially the bhikshunis and bhikshus.

- Refrain From Intoxicants

It doesn't matter if it is the internet, television, alcohol, or drugs; if anything clouds the mind, it doesn't help you see what a Buddhist being is all about.

This mainly means not partaking in alcoholic beverages. It can also involve not taking any stimulant type or anything that can cause you to conduct immoral behaviors or lose consciousness. Morphine, sniffing glue, huffing paint, amphetamines, opium, marijuana are all examples of things that you can't partake of.

The first four of these precepts constrain behaviors that might make you transgress or sin, so basically, they are just rules against deeds that are considered evil. Not drinking any alcohol is a precept since even though alcohol isn't a sin, it can cause you to lose your self-discipline, and you might commit a crime. This means that this last precept is a rule against any act that might keep you from looking out for other people's well being.

According to one story, a person in India drank alcohol and stole one of his neighbor's chickens. He then killed it and cooked it for food to eat while he drank his alcohol. Once his neighbor began looking for the chicken, he lied to her because he told her that he hadn't seen it. He noticed that his neighbor was very pretty, and he began sexually harassing her. Within this story, he violated every one of the precepts, and it all began with the last one.

Buddhism is one religion that puts a strong emphasis on wisdom, and when you don't drink, and you remain wise, clear-minded, and sober.

What Do the Five Precepts Mean?

Although there are five different precepts, their main principle is really not to offend anyone. When you don't offend others and only show them respect, they will be free. When you don't kill, you aren't causing harm to anybody's life. When you don't steal, you won't be trespassing on another's property. When you abstain from sexual misconduct, you aren't offending another person's integrity and honor. When you don't lie, you are offending another person's good name. When you don't drink or partake of other intoxicants, you won't be offending your intellect or anyone else's.

. . .

There is a common misconception that by taking on the precepts, you have to tie yourself down basically, and some people might say something like this: "Why observe the precepts? It is just too much of a burden." If you were to take the time to meet some people who are in jail, you might find that most of them have violated one or maybe all of the five precepts. Disfigurement, physical assault, and murder are all violations of the precept of no killing.

Abductions, kidnappings, robberies, theft, stealing, embezzlement, and corruption are all within the "no stealing" precept and are all violations of this precept. Bigamy, seduction, prostitution, and rape are violations of the "no sexual misconduct" precept. Intimidation, falsifying evidence, breaking promises, defamation, and libel are all ways you can violate the "no lying" precept. Drinking alcohol, smoking, drug trafficking, taking drugs, and dealing drugs are all ways you can violate the "no intoxicants" precept. It is because you have violated these precepts that you have lost your freedom. Therefore, you need to observe these precepts in a way that abides with your county, state, and government laws.

People who observe the five precepts and people who understand these precepts clearly will be able to enjoy true freedom. The true meaning of precept is freedom and not a burden.

. . .

It is believed that violating these precepts can be seen when taken; therefore, if you don't observe the precepts, you won't be making any violations. The truth is, even if you violate a precept after you take them, you will be filled with shame and will want to repent. Because of this, sin won't be as severe, and you will have a chance to reach enlightenment. But anyone who is reluctant to observe the precepts wouldn't feel the need to repent if they did violate the precepts, and they would have to stay in the "Three Evil Realms." "The Evil Realms" consist of animals, hungry ghosts, and hell; these people might never become a Buddha. If you decide not to take the precepts, it doesn't mean the precepts haven't been violated if you do something wrong because you are still guilty of whatever crime you committed and will need to bear their consequences.

If you don't kill and, in fact, protect lives, you will enjoy longevity and health. If you don't steal, but you generously give to the needy and poor, you will enjoy wealth and will be so honored. If you don't commit any form of sexual misconduct and respect other people's integrity and honor, you will have a harmonious family life. If you don't lie but praise other people, you will have a great reputation. If you don't partake of alcohol and stay away from intoxicants like drugs, you will have high awareness and a healthy body.

I think I have made it clear that numbers have a symbolic dimension in Buddhism. If we continue to ignore them, we remain blind to the meaning that the Buddhist texts give us. Since Buddhist traditions don't offer any keys to understanding these things, we have to realize how important numbers are used in various traditions, especially ancient ones.

Even though numbers began as concrete, and these bases can still be found in some texts, they have moved far away from the normal traditions. It is in this "emptiness" that numbers give us a blank canvas for projecting our dreams. Just like any other fundamental symbol, they have various meanings that will always be hard to define, but they speak to us in terms of our existence.

Numbers are a part of the universal language. The huge spectrum of numbers is a lot alike in most cultures, but what has been said about them might be a lot different. The symbolism of the number one is alike in Vedism and Buddhism, but one difference is that the Vedas want to return to the One; Buddhists want to let go of One, so they can realize the only try Buddhist number that is zero.

BUDDHIST PERFECTIONS

In Buddhism, paramita or parami refers to the perfections. These perfections are described in Buddhist texts as noble qualities that are associated with enlightened beings. There are two sets of perfections. There are three different lists of paramitas in Buddhist teachings. First is the ten perfections of Theravada, which were taken from several sources. Then there are the six perfections of Mahayana, and these were taken from several Mahayana Sutras, which includes the Lotus Sutra. The third is Bon. There are ten perfections in the Bon tradition. They are similar to Mahayana, but with some differences. We won't be talking about them, but I will list them for you in case you would like to know:

1. Generosity
2. Ethical self-discipline
3. Patience
4. Perseverance
5. Concentration or mental stability
6. Strengthening

7. Compassion
8. Aspirational prayer
9. Skill in means
10. Wisdom or discriminating awareness

*A*s you read through the chapter, you will notice that the Bon belief changes the order of several of the perfections; they add in compassion and remove deep awareness.

For those who are wrestling with the best way to practice Buddhism and dharma in life, the perfections provide them with a useful framework in which to develop a healthy attitude towards daily activities so that you undertake any relationship or activity wisely. Perfections are also one of the few reliable ways to measure the accomplishments in a person's life.

TEN PERFECTIONS OF THERAVADA

The qualities that the perfections describe are considered to be the qualities a person needs to reach Buddhahood. They have to be practiced diligently and to perfection. These ten paramis date back to early Buddhism. The act of reaching Buddhahood is only possible for bodhisattvas. While listeners of Buddha's teachings can aim for these perfections, they aren't considered far-reaching unless connected with a bodhichitta goal. These perfections are found several times in the Jataka Tales and the Sutta Pitaka. The order of the perfections is also important. Each quality will help lead to the next, so you have to start at the top in order to get to the tenth perfection.

BUDDHISM

1. Dana – Perfection of Giving

Once you have perfected generosity or giving, it is considered selfless. You no longer measure the gain or loss. No longer are their strings attached or any expectations of reciprocity or thanks. The simple act of giving is gratifying all on its own, and there is no amount of loss or reluctance during this act of giving. When a person gives in this unencumbered manner, it loosens the grip of greed, and it helps to develop non-attachment. This type of giving develops virtue and will naturally lead to the next perfection.

To attain this perfection, you have to understand what your motivation is. In the Sutta-Pitaka, there are lists of motivations for giving. These include being intimidated or shamed into giving, giving to feel good about yourself, and receiving favor. These are considered to be impure. You have to give without attaching yourself to the recipient of the gift. The act of giving is supposed to help release self-clinging and greed. Some teachers will say that giving is good because it created good karma that will bring you happiness in the future. Others say that even this would be considered self-clinging and an expectation of reward.

It's also important to understand giving can't happen without receiving, and no givers without receivers. Giving and receiving will happen together. One cannot occur without the other. Giving and receiving this understanding helps you to reach the perfection of giving. However, if you continuously sort yourself into the giver or receiver category, you are still falling of dana.

1. Sila – Perfection of Morality

While it is believed that moral actions will naturally flow after releasing selfish desires, it's also true that releasing selfish desires will naturally flow from moral actions. Throughout most of Asia, basic Buddhist practices for the layperson are practicing the Precepts and giving alms to monastics. The Precepts aren't just some random list of rules as much as they are principles that a person should apply to their life to live in harmony with others. Appreciation of the values of living in harmony and giving will lead to third perfection.

Morals tend to be a much-debated topic in most of the world. However, in Buddhism, there are no moral absolutes. It encompasses a wide array of practices and beliefs, and the scriptures provide some room for interpretations. This is all based on the idea that each person should analyze issues carefully for themselves. When you are making a choice, you need to examine your motivation and weigh the possible consequences. Within Buddhism, they use self-reflection, mindfulness, liturgy, and meditation to do this. While moral and ethical behavior in Buddhism is probably not perfect, it does have a higher success rate than that of any other religion.

In our 'rule' world, we associate morals with rules you have to follow. Buddhism does not see it as such. Buddhism does not believe a person should suffer from Buddhism. Unlike most mainstream religions, who preach about what is right and wrong and suffering is often seen as righteous, you won't find that within the moral code of Buddhism. There is no notion of 'you either follow the rules or hedonist with no moral compass' within

Buddhism. There are several different approaches to Buddhism, and they are personal choices.

1. Nekkhamma – Perfection of Renunciation

*I*n Buddhism, renunciation is explained as letting go of whatever binds you to ignorance and suffering. While this may sound simple, it is easier said than done. This is because the thing that binds us is things that we all think we have to have to experience happiness. The Buddha taught that true renunciation requires a thorough examination of the ways in which we make ourselves unhappy through greed. Once we have done this, surrender will naturally come, and it is a liberating and positive action and should not be seen or felt like a punishment. This leads you to the fourth perfection.

Renunciation is used a lot in Buddhist teachings. The strictest of definitions refers to the act of a nun or monk going forth into a homeless life so that they are free from lust. It is understood as letting go of things that bind you to suffer and ignorance in a more broad definition.

*I*t is believed that giving yourself over to sensual pleasure hinders enlightenment. Sensual desire is the first of the five hindrances to enlightenment that can be overcome through mindfulness. With mindfulness, you can see things for what they really are and accept the fact that going after sensual pleasure is only going to give you a temporary distraction from suffering or stress.

. . .

The act of renunciation is part of the Right Intention of the Eightfold Path—the people who choose to take part in monastic life discipline themselves to renounce the pursuit of pleasure. Most nuns and monks are celibate, and they live simple lives without personal possessions. Laypeople are not expected to give up their homes or to sleep under the trees. Instead, they are supposed to realize the ephemeral nature of belongings and not become attached to them.

1. Panna – The Perfection of Discerning Wisdom

As perfection, wisdom refers to seeing the true nature of the world. This means seeing the inherent impermanence and emptiness of everything. Wisdom also means you have a great understanding of the Four Noble Truths. This will then lead to the next perfection.

1. Virya – Perfection of Energy

Energy, also known as virya, refers to traversing the spiritual path with the determination and fearlessness of a warrior. You stick with the path no matter the obstacles you may cross. This type of fearlessness will naturally follow once you have reached wisdom. Once you have perfected and channeled energy, this effort will help to bring you to the next perfection.

Today, viraya is translated to the perfection of energy, the perfection of enthusiastic effort, and the perfection of zeal. It also has to do with heroic and courageous efforts. It is the exact opposite of defeatism and sloth. Virya can be about physical and mental energy. Taking care of your health is another aspect of this perfection. For most of us, the mental aspect is a bit harder. Most of us struggle to make time to practice this daily. Chanting or meditating is often the last thing we feel like doing after a long day.

It is explained that virya has three components. The first is the development of character. This is all about cultivating courage and having the will to walk your path no matter what. This could mean that you have to correct bad habits or give up making excuses. You may also find that you need to clear commitment to the path and cultivate confidence. The earliest Buddhist scholars describe this stage as cultivating the hardness of armor to face adversity.

The second aspect is spiritual training. It is all about taking your practice into your own hand and not depending only on the Sangha or even the practice. Part of spiritual training could include learning rituals and liturgy and studying Buddhist teachings.

The third aspect is practice for the benefit of others. This is what is known as bodhicitta, and means that you want to reach enlightenment in order to benefit others. This helps you to release selfish attachment.

1. Khanti – Perfection of Patience

Once you have developed the fearlessness and energy of a warrior, you will then be able to develop patience. Khanti translates to 'unaffected by' or 'able to withstand.' Some people may translate it to composure, endurance, tolerance, forbearance, or patience. In order to reach this perfection, you have to accept everything that happens with calmness and the understanding that whatever does happen is part of your spiritual path. This perfection helps us face any hardships we experience in life and the suffering created by others, even when you've reached out a helping hand.

In modern times, we may view this idea of ksanti as facing our difficulties in a constructive manner, instead of a destructive one. These difficulties could be disease and pain, loss of a loved one, or poverty. We learn how to stay strong and not be defeated by despair. In order to reach this, you have to accept the First Noble Truth, the truth of dukkha. We have to accept that life is going to be stressful and difficult, but it is also temporary. As we learn how to accept this, we also see the amount of energy and time we waste trying to deny or avoid dukkha.

Most of our reactions to suffering are self-protection. We want to avoid things that we believe are going to hurt us, and we think that we are experiencing something unfortunate when we experience pain.

1. Sacca – Perfection of Truthfulness

Once you have developed patience, you are better at speaking the truth, even when people aren't interested in hearing it. Truthfulness helps to bring about honesty and excellence, and it will help you to develop determination. This also means that you have to acknowledge the truth within yourself, and this will go hand-in-hand with developing your wisdom.

1. Adhitthana – Perfection of Determination

Determination helps us understand what we need to reach enlightenment and give it your complete focus and help ignore or eliminate anything that gets in your way. It is a resolve to continue following your path no matter what you may have to face. Having this clear path will help you to develop loving-kindness.

1. Metta – Perfection of Loving Kindness

Loving-kindness is a mental state that can only be found through lots of practice. It will require deliberate and a complete abandonment of self-centeredness so that you can understand that the suffering of others is also your suffering. Perfecting metta is an essential part of getting rid of self-clinging that keeps you bound to suffering. Metta is the only antidote to fear, anger, and selfishness.

A big misunderstanding people have when it comes to Buddhists and metta is that Buddhists have always to be nice. Typically, niceness is only a social construct. Being nice has to do with self-preservation and keeping a sense of belonging within your social group. We only act nice because we want others to like us, or at the very least, not get angry with us. While, for the most part, there is nothing wrong with being nice, it isn't the same thing as metta. Metta is all about the genuine happiness of others. Often, when a person is acting badly, the last thing they need to reach happiness is for a person to enable their actions politely. Sometimes a person needs to hear something that they don't want to.

Sometimes they have to be shown that how they are acting is not right.

Metta is talked about in the Metta Sutta, or sutra, in the Sutta Pitaka. It gives you three ways to practice loving-kindness—the first is to apply it to your daily conduct. The second is through Metta meditation. The third is committing to embody Metta with your mind and body. The third naturally comes from the first two.

1. Upekkha – Perfection of Equanimity

*E*quanimity means that you can impartially see things without the influence of your ego or tyranny. When you have equanimity, you no longer get pulled this way and that by your dislikes, passions, and likes.

*W*hile upekkha is often translated to equanimity, the precise meaning is hard to figure out; one translation has it as 'to look over.' Another gives the translation as 'not taking notice; to disregard.' According to Bhikku Bodhi, a Theravadin monk, the word has previously been mistranslated as 'indifference,' which has made a lot of people believe that Buddhists are supposed to be detached and unconcerned with other things. The truth is, you are not supposed to be ruled by likes, passions, or dislikes.

It is also easy to turn to the life of Buddha for guidance. After he reached enlightenment, he definitely didn't live within a state of indifference. He actually spends 45 years actively teaching the idea of dharma to other people.

. . .

The Theravada tradition explains that each of these perfections has three levels, ordinary, medium, and highest. For example, to reach the highest level of generosity, a bodhisattva would give their body for others to eat. In a past life as a rabbit, if a beggar asked him for food, the Buddha would throw himself onto a fire so that the man would no longer be starving.

SIX PERFECTIONS OF MAHAYANA

These six perfections are paramitas that Mahayana Buddhist study and practice. These virtues are supposed to be cultivated to help strengthen a person's practice and help them to reach enlightenment. This enlightenment in the Mahayana tradition is not too different from the Theravada tradition and means that you have reached your own true Buddha-nature. If it doesn't seem to be your true nature, then the perfections are still obscured by fear, greed, anger, or delusion.

Some of the most popular commentaries of these six perfections are located in Arya Sura's *Paramitasamasa* and *Bodhicaryavatara*. Later on, the Mahayana Buddhists added four more, which included skillful means, aspiration, spiritual power, and knowledge, to create a list of ten. However, it is more common for people to study and develop the original six than it is for them to use the list of ten.

. . .

Like with the other list of perfections, each perfection supports the other, so you have to reach them in order.

Also, the first three perfections are virtuous practice for anybody to have. The last three specifically deal with a person's spiritual practice.

1. Dana Paramita – Perfection of Generosity

In a lot of writings about these perfections, it is said that generosity is an entryway to dharma. Generosity is where bodhicitta starts, which is the aspiration to realize enlightenment for everything. This is critically important to the Mahayana Buddhists. Dana paramita is a true generosity of your spirit. It means that you give with the sincere desire to help others without expecting anything in return. For it to be true generosity, selfishness cannot be attached. Doing charity to 'feel good about me' does not count as dana paramita.

1. Sila Paramita – Perfection of Morality

In Buddhism, morality isn't all about having unquestioning obedience to a set of rules. They may have their precepts; they work more like training wheels instead of rules. They are there to help guide us until we have discovered balance. An enlightened being can respond correctly to every situation without needing to turn to a list of rules. When it comes to practicing sila paramita, you will develop selfless compassion. During this time, you will also practice renunciation and will gain more appreciation for karma.

BUDDHISM

1. Kasanti Paramita – Perfection of Patience

Ksanti refers to composure, endurance, forbearance, tolerance, or patience. It is believed that there are three dimensions to reach this level of patience. They are the ability to endure hardships, patience with others, and acceptance of the truth. To reach perfection, you have to start out by accepting the Four Noble Truths, which includes the truth of suffering. Through practice, your attention will move from your suffering, and towards the suffering others are experiencing. Accepting truth means that you accept difficult truths about yourself, like we are mortal or greedy, and accept the truth that our existence is an illusion.

1. Virya Paramita – Perfection of Energy

Virya refers to zeal or energy. This comes from the old Indian-Iranian word that means 'hero' and acts as the root word for 'virile.' This means that virya paramita is all about making a heroic and courageous effort to realize enlightenment. In order to reach this, you will have to develop your courage and character. You have to engage in spiritual training and then use your fearless efforts to help out other people.

1. Dhyana Paramita – Perfection of Meditation

Dhyana is a Buddhist meditation and is a discipline that is meant to cultivate the mind. Dhyana translates to 'concentration,' and in this context, a lot of concentration is applied to reaching insight and clarity. A very close word to dhyana is Samadhi, which also translates to 'concentration.' Samadhi is about single-pointed concentration where all sense of self is released. Both words are said to be the basic foundation of wisdom, which is the last perfection.

1. Prajna Paramita – Perfection of Wisdom

Within the Mahayana Buddhist belief system, wisdom is the intimate and direct realization of emptiness or sunyata. In the simplest of terms, this is the teaching that every phenomenon is without independent existence or self-essence. The idea that everything is without self-essence may seem very wise, but as you work through the teachings of prajna, sunyata's significance starts to be more evident. The importance of this within Mahayana cannot be stressed enough. This sixth paramita represents transcendent knowledge, where there is no longer a battle between self and other.

KARMA

ONE OF THE fundamental principles of Buddhism is the law of karma. In the simplest of terms, karma refers to the idea that all intentional actions will come with consequences in your current and future lives. In fact, it is your karma that will dictate your rebirths. Buddhists understand that the law of karma is another manifestation of the law of cause and effect. This is where everything that exists comes from certain conditions. In this way, karma law can be seen as a natural law so that actions are followed by a consequence, not because of some divine judgment. Buddha stressed that actions would lead to an inevitable appropriate consequence.

Many people toss the word karma around a lot to explain any event that they can't explain. However, they don't reflect on what they actually mean. It sometimes seems that it is just another way to say, "It was fate," or "It was meant to be." It has become this mysterious or impersonal force that shapes our life. Karma originated in India and has been a big part of

India's religious tradition. Karma isn't some mysterious thing to them and is any consequence or effect that comes from actions a person takes. The effects of karma can show up throughout your lifetime, depending on the good or evil deeds that created the outcome.

As this idea was expanded upon, it became inseparable from the idea of Transmigration. This is their belief that people undergo several rebirths, which you will learn about in the next chapter. The forms that these rebirths take are based on one's karma. They felt as though their beliefs were true because of the molting of snakes. They were shedding old skin for a new one.

Karma is like the ultimate justice in life. The type of life a person is born into and how they develop throughout their life is seen as the result of their choices in one of their previous lives. Karma and rebirth are used to explain why some people are born disabled, are prodigies, if they are from the upper or lower class, among other things.

The idea of karma and rebirth quickly spread throughout Asia because it helped to answer the perplexing issue of suffering. It also moved beyond the whimsy of gods who's maliciousness or anger was always unpredictable. It also ruled out miracles because everything ran by the cause of an effective rule. Rather, they had a moral law that the universe controlled and was rooted within the belief of cause and effect. This is also a popular belief as it appeals to a person's self-benefit and self-interest as a means to cause good behavior. It is all based on the whole pleasure-pain response. Everybody is going to choose the pleasure of pain in the long run.

When you build up enough good karma, it can mean that they will face good fortune in their afterlife.

The actual idea about karma is much more complicated and complex than our understanding. How does our karma come into being? In Buddhism, karma may be handed out in the very next life a person lives, or it may not happen for many other lives after, and it could be coming from an indeterminate past. You could look at the maturity of karma like a seed that lays dormant until the conditions of sun and moisture are just right to start the germination process. This can be seen in human life as children don't mature until the right time.

Karma will also deal with conditions. Once specific conditions have been reached, then the karmic consequence can occur. While most people will view this idea of karma as fate, especially when you look at it in hindsight, Buddhism does not accept the idea of fatalism. Buddhism fully believes that you can change your karma whenever you want. Bad karma can be counteracted, as can good karma. It can also be moderated by creating good conditions that stop the growth of bad karma. Based on free will, Buddhism tells us that bad karma can be overcome. That makes the idea of karma positive.

One of the most interesting things about this belief system is that it takes away one of humanity's most popular defense mechanisms in life, which is the victim mentality. When things aren't going your way, do you sometimes feel down on yourself and start going through a list of circumstances or people you can place the blame on? Perhaps you said something means to someone at work, and when you were confronted about it with your boss, you explain how other people have treated you, the stress of a bigger workload than usual, something the person said or did which set you off.

*H*ow often do you see people stand straight up and take 100% of the responsibility for their harmful actions? Especially when people are watching them or keeping tabs. Those who make a concerted effort at responsibility with the principle of karma in their minds believe that this contributes to the success they experience throughout their time on earth. This idea is reflected in many other Western social ideals, such as the saying that if you work hard enough, you can achieve anything. Though not a karmic concept, it does encourage the idea that you get out of life what you put in, which a lot of people agree to be true.

*K*arma is not restricted to Buddhist thought and comprises a foundational belief system in Hinduism. Hinduism's karma principles describe three different forms; sanchita karma, prarabdha karma, and kriyamana karma. Each of these forms represents a certain aspect of the karma that is present in each individual's life.

*S*anchita karma describes all of the karma that has accumulated in a person's past and has yet to come to a resolution. You might think of a person who is followed around by a huge cloud of energy that has been created from his/her past actions and has yet to manifest effects in a person's life. A kind of account that is filled and dispersed at a slower rate than is invested into it. This isn't a perfect metaphor, of course, but it helps put a little more of a visual aide into the thought process. Everything you say and do in this life results in energy creation; it is a positive and negative presence that then has to dissipate within your life at another point in time. You must "pay" for this creation in some way, whether you've brought it about directly or indirectly. Think of the scientific law that states that "for every action, there is an equal and opposite reaction." It's just that with karma, those reactions are more ethereal and are unable to be observed directly and immediately.

The second form, prarabdha karma, represents the karma that you have not yet experienced but is on its way. This idea puts a timeline on things to separate what has happened in the past and what will happen in the future. The message is that there is no escaping karma; it will manifest in your life once your actions have created it.

The third and final form is called kriyamana karma, and this represents the karma that you are actively creating in the present, which will manifest as future karma. So there is a triad of past, present, and future, essentially illustrating that karma is present at every time and point in our lives. From the moment we are born, we begin creating and stirring the pot of these energies and potentialities in the form of karma, creating and trapping ourselves into its influence with every breath we take. Thinking of life from this point of view really closes in on the personal responsibility concept! Think of the contrast between Eastern and Western thought in this area, where our sin can essentially be "erased" through God's divine love and sacrifice through a simple acceptance of salvation through confession in the Catholic tradition. Whereas in Eastern thought, your actions follow you throughout your life, not allowing for any kind of escape from your responsibility as a human being to uphold the eightfold path and be constantly on the move toward enlightenment and divine-human understanding.

LIBERATING POTENTIAL

When Buddha was alive, most religions in India taught their followers that karma operated in a simple straight line. This line was that past actions influenced the present; present behaviors influenced the future. To Buddhists, though, karma is non-linear and very complex. It acts within several feedback looks, with our present being shaped by the present and past actions. We do today not only affect our future selves, but it can also affect the present moment.

While the past does influence your present, you can also shape your present through your actions now. This is what makes karma liberating. You have the power to change how things are going to turn out for you by doing good and building up good karma. Who you are and where you came from isn't as important as your mind's current motives. While the past can account for some inequalities you see in life, the measure of your worth is not from the hand you have been dealt with because you have the power to change that at any time.

TWO MEANINGS OF KARMA

There are two basic meanings of karma, and we'll refer to them as universal and psychological. For the western Buddhists, they only have one meaning in mind, and that is the psychological meaning. The psychological meaning is the intentional action of the body, mind, and speech that creates a consequence. For example, suppose you made a habit of going to the monastery and giving money and food to the nuns and monks. In that case, generosity will have certain consequences. You will likely feel happier, inspired, and your life will likely have more meaning.

Conversely, if you often stole packets of coffee from work, then you are going to face certain consequences. You would likely be unhappier as you are worried that the kitchen manager at work may find out. You may also feel that your life is a struggle because you can't relax into every moment with a clear conscience.

This is the definition of karma that is the most important to understand when practicing Buddhism. This is the best basis to have to further your progress on the Buddhist path. It's also important to understand that while Buddhist ethics are based on the idea that "actions have consequences," good actions will have good consequences for everybody and not just for yourself.

However, there is a second meaning of karma. When Buddhists talk about karma law, they are likely thinking of something different, which we call universal karma. This is a more traditional meaning, and it is connected to the theory of universal moral justice. In this definition, the mind, body, and speech's intentional actions will have consequences in this life, or, more likely, in future lives. Suppose you go back to the example from earlier where you have a habit of going to the monastery and giving money and food. In that case, this is going to create merit, which is like a positive balance in the universe. Once you die, it will come to fruition in you having a pleasant rebirth, possibly into a well-off family or within a heavenly realm. But suppose you are stealing those coffee packets, after you die. In that case, you could have a less pleasant rebirth, possibly into a family of thieves, hell-realm, or even in a family of coffee growers.

This definition of karma is part of Buddhist cosmology. Since there is universal impermanence, everything is born and dies constantly, and the effects of good and bad deeds only last for a certain period before they are exhausted. This is why gods could fall, and the people in hell could find a way back into the day. This is cosmic justice, whereby your moral acts never go away but are woven into the fabric of reality.

A belief in karma has the power to improve the social and financial conditions of an order. Giving to the monks has long been seen as the best way to build up good karma. Followers are encouraged to do good deeds on behalf of the deceased to send them extra good karma to them so that they can earn a better rebirth. This is why many Buddhist monasteries and temples have always been wealthy and owned vast tracts of land. They have also inspired amazing art that the entire world admires without looking at such work's social cost. People believe that keeping up a priestly order will help create harmony within the universe and make a space of peace and prosperity.

When the Mahayana tradition emerged, they experienced a change in understanding. It went from metaphysical to religious. The goal was to become Buddha instead of individually reaching Nirvana and gaining release from karmic suffering. With Mahayana teachings, Buddhahood's goal meant that you would eventually be one with the force that works to be salvation to everything. It turned into something altruistic.

When it came to the ordinary people, karma and rebirth stayed the same. People could move through different realms. Karma dictated each person's attainment. Depending on what a person's karma was, they could ascend or descend. When they are human, they once again have the chance to work towards enlightenment and remove themselves from this karmic process.

OTHER FORCES AT PLAY

Buddhism will also tell you that there are many other forces at play other than karma that will help to shape your life. These include natural forces like gravity and the seasons. If a natural disaster, like an earthquake, hits a town, this isn't some form of collective karmic punishment. It is simply an unfortunate event that needs compassion in response and not judgment.

There are a lot of people who have a hard time understanding that your actions form karma. This could be because they were raised with other religious models, and they are looking to believe that there is some type of mysterious cosmic force directing karma, rewarding the good, and punishing the bad. This is what real Buddhism is about. It's important to understand that karma isn't some type of "moral justice" or "reward and punishment." These ideas are based on the idea of a supreme being, a God, who sits in judgment, who makes rules and laws, and decides what is wrong and what is right. The word justice is a dangerous and ambiguous one and can do much more harm than good. Just remember, karma is cause and effect; it is natural and has nothing to do with justice.

FINDING GOOD KARMA

If you are intrigued by these concepts and enjoy trying to wrap your mind around them with understanding, you have already taken your first important steps into the world and meditation benefits. Meditation and the pursuit of deeper understanding begin when we are awakened to realize that there is more to life than living like a robot, going about our daily lives without really thinking about our presence in the world or our purpose within it. When life is all about paying bills and getting "the job done," we avoid having to think too deeply about ourselves. A lot of people are happy to continue through life this way because it means they aren't really giving themselves time to think about the darker realities of existence and the darker parts of themselves. Perhaps they are working along this road in hopes that they will simply be blindsided by death, and it will all be over before they even realize it. This is the ultimate form of evasion of life, and many people would say this is not even really living. As human beings, we are unique in our capacity to think, wonder, and be amazed and inspired. At the very least, human life is naturally geared toward some degree of curiosity and a drive to progress in some way. Humans are not designed to be satisfied with inactivity for long. The human mind is a tragic thing to go to waste if we choose to blindly live as if we are no more than cats and dogs. We are not cats and dogs, and so it is imperative that to find any source of happiness and satisfaction in this short life, we must begin at some point to look inward and take a step back from our outside lives to think a moment about what life is on a deeper level. This, in itself, is meditation.

. . .

There are a thousand different methods and techniques of meditation, but don't be overwhelmed with the idea that there is a "right" and "wrong" way to meditate. I believe that simply sitting there reading these words is a form of meditation as you put outside influences on hold and let your mind wander over new and inspiring concepts. As you become stronger in your skill and practice, you are welcome to delve deeper into any tradition and methodology that captures your interest, and there is a huge volume of resources to be tapped into when you are ready.

REBIRTH

DURING THE PROCESS of reaching Nirvana, Buddha was said to have recognized all of his previous lives. He also stated that anything from one life would move to the next.

Buddhists know life as samsara, which means to wander forever. He described this transition as a billiard ball hitting against another billiard ball. Even though nothing physical transfers from one to the other, the second ball's direction and speed directly relate to the first one. The term that Buddhists use most is rebirth instead of reincarnation. Reincarnation implies that a person's essence or soul gets transferred. Rebirth uses a law of causality since it happens due to circumstances that happened before.

The main goal for Buddhists is to break free from samsara and to reach Nirvana.

WHAT IS NIRVANA?

Nirvana is a term that most people misunderstand in Buddhism. People in the West see it as meaning Heaven or achieving Heaven on Earth or maybe even a rock band.

No doubt, you are not completely unfamiliar with this term, as it is thrown around all over the place in popular culture, music, TV, and lots of books. Nirvana is the word that represents the state of enlightenment and that space where there is a complete absence of suffering, where the principle of impermanence is fully embraced. The illusion of duality falls away completely.

There is a common misconception out there that Nirvana is a place or a destination. Some people might say that this Nirvana might be kind of like heaven from the Christian doctrines, where there are milk and honey and lots of beautiful things around. But this is an inaccurate assumption. Nirvana is not a place but a state of mind, as described above. It is in this state of mind that the individual experiences profound peace and the absence of suffering.

It is notable that the Buddha, in his teachings, never spent a lot of words on trying to describe or teach others about what exactly Nirvana is. It is said that Nirvana's idea or reality is far beyond whatever words we could ever use to try to describe it. It is far beyond this earthly realm of things and objects and metaphors, etc. This, in itself, is a useful tool for you to use in your meditation, even at the beginning. Try to wrap your mind around what Nirvana is, to you, and to the classic Buddhism teachers and students. The object here is not to come to a perfect understanding but to focus your mind on a concept and use this focus as a way to practice moving your mind to a place of calm. Remember, it's not about shutting down the mind, but about reigning it into a place where there is quiet and peace and wisdom. This will come with time and practice.

Buddha says Nirvana is a Buddhist's ultimate goal. He reached it during his enlightenment. From that point on, he decided to teach other people about it to experience everything that he experienced. Upon his death, 45 years later, he passed through to Nirvana.

Nirvana basically means unbinding or extinguishing. It implies that it gives you freedom from whatever was binding you, like ignorance, jealousy, or desire's passion. When these things have been overcome, you will reach a state of bliss, and there won't be any need for the cycle of birth and death. Every one of your karmic debts will be paid.

Buddha refused to worry about what happened then but implied that it was without boundaries, and no words could describe it. He did see it was a totally different state than our normal existence and wasn't parallel to a person's rebirth.

WHAT IS REBIRTH?

Buddhists believe that when they die, they get reborn, and this process of death and rebirth continues until they finally reach Nirvana. This brings up the question: "What is the person?" Many religions think that any person's core, their real selves, is their soul or an eternal entity that will live on in the afterlife. Buddhism states that a person is made up of perceptions, feelings, and thoughts that interact with their body in an ever-changing, dynamic way. When they die, this mental energy gets re-established into another body. In this way, Buddhism can explain a person's continuity without having to believe in a soul. This idea contradicts impermanence, which is a Universal Truth. Various Buddhist traditions will explain this process differently. Some say that rebirth happens right after you die; some say that it will take 49 days. Some people think there is an intermediate place and others say there isn't. Everyone agrees that the circumstances around rebirth get conditioned by the total amount of karma that they created in another life.

People who criticize Buddhism say that if there isn't a soul, but just a stream of mental energy that is constantly changing, there can't be an identity and talking about a person being reborn or experiencing bad or good actions that they did in the past doesn't mean anything. But this criticism doesn't understand identity in change. In just one single life, we can see a person changing. Sometimes this can be very drastic, but we can still recognize them as being the same person. This happens since various aspects of this person changes at different rates. Their complexion or the number of wrinkles on their face might change as they get older, but the overall shape of their face won't change that much. A person can change their beliefs while still holding onto them with the same intensity as they held their other beliefs. They might hold onto their former beliefs but less intensely than before. Let's look at an example: Take the Ganges River. It is constantly changing each moment, and over hundreds of years, its course, width, quality, and quantity of water have changed, but it is still recognized as being the same exact river.

. . .

Other people claim that rebirth wasn't part of Buddha's original teachings or that he copied this idea about rebirth from the Hindu concept of reincarnation. All the evidence can contradict both of these claims. Rebirth is a concept found in the earliest records of Buddha's teachings that were preserved in the Pali Tipitaka. There isn't any evidence of it being added later on. Looking at some of the earlier Hindu literature shows their idea about rebirth or reincarnation wasn't accepted. It wasn't mentioned in either the Brahmana Sutras or the Vedas. Some Upansads continue to teach it while others condemn it. The idea was around before Buddha, but it wasn't accepted, and it wasn't a part of orthodox Hinduism. This is something that happened a lot later, due to the result of Buddha's influence.

THE TRUTH ABOUT REBIRTH

Every time you choose between two different things, you make a type of wager as to the consequences of your choice. This can be seen more when you are choosing between something that would have a pleasant reward that won't last very long or something hard that gives you a lot of reward after a certain amount of time. Is the harder choice going to be worth it? Will the easy on be irresponsible? As a person who is embedded within time, there isn't a way to know for certain.

You have to think about some particulars in your future. Will you, or some of your loved ones, live long enough to get to feel the results of your actions? Could something interfere and wipe out everything that you did?

· · ·

Then you have to think about the bigger uncertainties in life: Do we have any real control over our actions, or are all of the things we do predetermine by something powerful being? If we have a choice, is it worthwhile to face the hard ones? Does any of this really matter? If the choices we make matter, then how far into the future are we going to need to calculate their consequences? Will they only affect our current life or shape the lives of future people once we pass on?

Any type of argument based on reason or logic has not concluded these problems. Likewise, the religions of the world don't agree on an answer. Even empirical science can't tell what the answer is. But everyone keeps grappling with these questions. We aren't happy with the answer, 'I don't know,' yet we also refuse to give them much thought. Even deciding not to gives these questions much thought is a wager that really doesn't matter.

When Buddha came about, he taught us that these things do matter, and enlightenment gives us perspective on the way these choices work in different dimensions. You will come to understand that every choice you make is real, that they can make big differences in your life, and the consequences can shape this life but will also shape several lifetimes. If your mind still craves things after your rebirth, you will die and be reborn again and again. Before your enlightenment, you won't understand these things as a certainty, but Buddha explained that if you are planning on reaching enlightenment and lessen your suffering, it is smarter to assume that these things are hypotheses.

This basically means that as long as you haven't reached enlightenment, this will also be a wager. The reason for this chapter on rebirth is to show why when you repeatedly put a wager on your actions, the best course of action is to put all your bets on him.

THE ANCIENT CONTROVERSY

It's a bit difficult to understand why modern scholars continue to repeat this idea that everybody believed in rebirth during the time Buddha was living. The Pali gives us clear evidence that contradicts this. The evidence has been available to the Western languages for over 100 years.

Buddha talked about the two opposites of a bad view that can block a person's progress on their path: annihilationism and eternalism. Annihilation is a term that he used to describe the people who didn't believe in rebirth. He didn't invent this term as other teachers would accuse him of being an annihilationist, too.

There are some passages that show a colorful way that annihilationism was shared during his time. They talked about two famous annihilationists. Ajita Kesakambalin was the first, and he was the leader of a group of materialists. The other was Prince Payasi. He held some similar materialistic views that were similar to Ajita's. He used his powers to kill criminals. He used this chance to perform some horrible experiments to see if there were any areas of the human body that could survive death. He shared these experiments with the Buddhist monk Kumara Kassapa.

. . .

BUDDHISM

A more comprehensive picture of annihilationist views classified them, by the way, they defined self-annihilation at death. They had a total of seven kids. Three explained the person as a body, which could be referred to as either a physical body that was composed of four material elements, an astral body, or a divine physical body. The views of Ajita and the Prince fall under the first one. Others would define the self as being formless and experience dimensions of nothingness, infinite space, neither perception nor infinite consciousness.

*F*or any of the non-Buddhist schools that talk about rebirth, the Pali names four: Jains, Brahmans, and two Samana schools. One of the schools was led by Pakudha Kaccayana, and the other by Makkhali Gosala. We know that the Brahmans and Jains affirmed that all actions would play a part in shaping your rebirth. The Canon states that there are teachers who denied action plays a part in a person's rebirth.

*O*ther than the exponents that we named above, there are also several kinds of views that it talks about, and that is 'partial eternalists' and 'eternalists.' Eternalists said that the soul wasn't changed during the rebirth process. Partial eternalists said that some people would undergo a change in their position in the Universe and how they experienced pain and pleasure as they went through their various lives. Others say that the soul doesn't change its position at all.

. . .

Even though the Pali doesn't talk about these theories in a lot of detail, we understand through other sources that the Brahmans and Jains did a lot to define the kind of essence or self that would be reborn. You can find the most details about what a soul is in the Brahmanical Upanisads. They discuss many of the theories about the things that can be reborn. They explain that the self will become conscious and leave the body. This 'self' will be an immortal breath-energy and won't have a body. It is the underlying force within the Universe. Our minds can detect the supreme self that is located in an astral body.

They also record various descriptions about the soul's progress after we die; the most interesting one divides the living into three groups. Those in developed classes go to Brahman once they die. The middle-class people will go in stages to the moon, and they eat the moon. They will then come back to earth in the form of rain and will transform into plants. Then they get reborn as an animal that eats the plants. The animals which have good karma will get eaten by humans. The ones with bad karma will get eaten by all kinds of other animals. The lowest class that included insects will suffer a fate that could not be described.

It is easy to see that discussing rebirth, everybody will have a different stand on the two problems. The first is the person's nature and then an explanation of the way they were or weren't annihilated when they died. Basically, each side of things felt as though they needed to explain their position by taking some sort of stand about the metaphysics of people's identity.

• • •

The second problem was the relationship between the actions of humans and their rebirth. It doesn't matter if the course of rebirth gets affected by their actions or not.

Because there is such a huge view on both sides, it is obvious that rebirth wasn't just an assumption that was never looked at within the Indian culture. During Buddha's life, this was the biggest controversial topic.

CHOOSING DISPASSION TO REACH NIRVANA

Since we all enjoy the passion, it's hard to make a choice to take a path that will lead us to dispassion. It requires a lot of motivation to take that path and to stick with it. At the same time, you have to make sure you stick to high standards because it's easy to fall into the trap of subtle passion that can end up sending you back to a life of rebirth and suffering. This is why you will find the correct views at the beginning of your path.

Conviction in rebirth plays an important role in motivating your initial choice to take this path and guiding the choice you make. Some think that believing in rebirth is some form of complacency. Basically, you are going to have many different lives to take on this path, so you should do it in your own time. However, Buddha explains that there are dangers in the rebirth process that gives you a different picture. You might die at any moment, and there are lots of different lives that you could find yourself in where it would be impossible to take this path. Even if you do end up getting reborn into a good level, the odds of a good rebirth after that aren't that good. That's why you must master the path while you can.

. . .

It is possible to reach the end of suffering in only one lifetime. You can find a lot of stories about people who reached an awakening after just one story from Buddha and made a choice to take the path to Nirvana. But that is only in principle. Every person who experiences awakening is going to have a different experience, and Buddha understood that. He understood that most of his listeners would take several lifetimes to fulfill this journey. There was a good chance that his listeners, like the rest of us, noticed the struggles of their lives and saw that they weren't going to have the time in this life to devote it to this path fully.

Buddha didn't make this path easier to accomplish within one lifetime, but, instead, he encouraged them to take a multi-life perspective. This was to convince them that whatever efforts they made during this life to reach awakening wasn't all for nothing. He kept the bar high, and this was for a good reason. Only once you have realized what this path is going to involve can you get anywhere worthwhile.

Buddha also went on to encourage people who were very close to death to do their best to create dispassion for other realms of rebirth. He said that it was possible for people to reach full awakening by doing this. This would help to keep them from facing future suffering and pain. A person who assumed only one lifetime would get them to Nirvana would not see the value of their efforts.

Besides providing a person with the motivation to practice the path, this belief in rebirth and karma plays big role in releasing our attachment to physical things. For example, if you don't think that something small could create huge repercussions in your life later on, and you want to enjoy it right now, you could see it as insignificant and allow it to affect your path. Only once you start to understand the possibility of some tiny little attachment to create long-term suffering will you willingly work towards abandoning them. That is the only time when you can follow that path.

BRINGING BUDDHISM INTO YOUR LIFE

BUDDHISM HAS MORE than 500 million followers, and it is one of the oldest religions that is still being practiced to this day. Buddhism has many different definitions, but it does have a set of values that can help you realize what Buddhism actually stands for.

As you know, Buddhism began more than 2000 years ago, when Siddhartha Gautama sat down underneath that ancient tree in Nepal and began meditating. This is where he found enlightenment and where Buddha was born.

PRACTICING BUDDHISM TO HAVE A HAPPY, PEACEFUL, AND MINDFUL LIFE

Buddhism isn't a religion like any of the others. It doesn't teach us about the importance of spiritual laws but about how a new way of life can change our personal lives.

Even though there are different groups of Buddhists, there is an understanding that everyone respects their beliefs. So, why do people decide to practice Buddhism?

Although there are many reasons, the main one is that you understand that every creature is familiar with suffering. This means that your life needs to be about relieving this suffering through kindness and openness.

Here are some ways you can learn to practice Buddhism:

Live With the Four Bodhisattva Vows

- Try to End Other People's Suffering

Buddhism teaches about the 'Four Noble Truths,' and these tell us that life and suffering are part of each other.

The only way to end suffering is to break out of your life's cycle of birth, death, and rebirth. You have to work towards helping other people with their physical and mental suffering. In order to accomplish this, you have to reach enlightenment. This can only be achieved by living within the 'Eightfold Path.'

- Following the Eightfold Path

This is the path that leads you to enlightenment. Enlightenment is a state of bliss where suffering can't live. We've covered these above, but here is a quick reminder:

- Right Action, Right Livelihood, Right Speech or the Five Precepts
- Right Mindfulness, Right Effort, Right Concentration or Meditation
- Right Understanding, Right Thought this includes the Five Precepts, Mindfulness, and Meditation

- Sever The Ties of Need and Desire

The majority of our lives get dictated by our wants and needs. We might want a new car, the largest house we can find, but it goes against everything that Buddhism stands for when we crave these material things.

- Learning Throughout Your Life

You can never think that you have learned all that you need to. Learning needs to be a lifetime goal, and the more you learn, the closer you will get to enlightenment.

Basically, we have to learn the dharma and how it relates to suffering.

Live Your Life By the Five Precepts

Again we have covered these in an earlier chapter, but you have to live by these in order to reach enlightenment, which is every Buddhist goal.

. . .

These might sound like the Ten Commandments to you, but they are different because they aren't rules that came from an almighty God but are more of a foundation on which to base your life so you can become the best version of yourself.

If you can follow these precepts, you can reach enlightenment and have the best life when you get reborn.

Live Your Life With Dharma and Karma

- Dharma

Dharma is the world's and your reality. Dharma is constantly changing and can be changed by interacting and seeing the world and all the choices you make.

You could think about dharma as understanding the tenants and paths of Buddhism or how you follow a Buddhist lifestyle. The easiest way to incorporate dharma into your life is to learn how to live in the moment and love the life you already have. You have to be thankful, grateful and spend each day working toward enlightenment.

- Karma

Karma is the main element when living a Buddhist lifestyle. It is the basic belief that all the things you do can be weighed as either 'bad' or 'good,' and your karma gets judged when your life does end.

. . .

If you have positive karma, you get reborn into a better life. If you have negative karma, you will get reborn into a life that is a lot worse than the one you are living now.

If your current life's circumstances get determined by your previous life's karma, this means that the only way you can make sure you have a better life the next time around, you have to be a very good person now.

The main differences between bad and good actions are the motivations that you have behind these actions. Good actions are always motivated by kindness, and you have a genuine desire to help relieve other people's suffering. Bad actions get motivated by greed, hatred, and consistent acts that bring other people's suffering.

Meditation

In order to reach Nirvana, you have to practice meditation each day to increase your openness and mindfulness. Meditation lets you be at one with your suffering and inner peace, and it is the first step toward reaching enlightenment.

Meditating is more than just sitting quietly while being lost in your own thoughts. Here is a quick guide to help you get used to meditating:

1. Find a space that is quiet and where you won't be disturbed. Get rid of all distractions like computers,

televisions, or your phone. Quiet music in the background can help calm the mind.
2. Sit down and get comfortable. Sit in a criss-cross applesauce position if it works for you; if not, just get comfortable. This position needs to be something where you forget about your body. Keep your spine straight but stay relaxed.
3. Focus. Many people like closing their eyes, but you don't have to. You could opt to just focus on a picture or spot to help you find inner peace. If you want to keep your eyes open, lower your gaze and fix it on an object in front of you.
4. Notice your breathing. You have to focus on each breath. Notice the air going out of and coming into your body. See how each breath feels. Notice the weight every push puts on your chest. Let yourself go.
5. Allow your thoughts to flow. Don't let your mind think about any one thing. Try your best to make your mind go blank and allow it to wander without any direction.

Try to do this for at least 15 minutes each day for one week. You need to use the same room and in the same position during this time. If you like meditating and want to continue doing it, make sure you extend your time by five minutes each week until you reach 45 minutes. You can use a timer so you won't have any temptation to stop and check the time on a clock.

WAYS YOU CAN INTEGRATE BUDDHISM INTO YOUR LIFE

People have been drawn to Buddhism for many reasons. The most compelling is the increased peace of mind, serenity, wanting to be a better person, and connecting to one's self better. But, there are times when we feel disconnected from life. Here are some ways that can help you integrate and apply Buddhism to your life:

- Keep In Mind That We Are One

The world's illusion can make us believe that we are all separate beings, but this can breed competition, mistrust, and fear. But, Buddhism tells us that everyone is just one facet of the Universe's consciousness. If you hurt another person, you are hurting yourself. You need to try to see others and the world in this way each day. Understand that there is just infinite Oneness, and you need to treat everybody as yourself.

- Say the Metta Prayer Each Day

This is the best way to commit to a Buddhist lifestyle to be kind to our intentions and thoughts. Saying this prayer can bring good wishes and positive energy to everyone beginning with yourself and your closest friends and family. This prayer's essence says: 'May all beings be free, peaceful, well, and happy.' This is a wonderful gift that we can give the world daily.

- Watch The State of Your Mind

Our minds are usually active and, at times, intrusive. Emotions and thoughts come and go like clouds floating across the sky. Sometimes our mind can be stormy, and at other times there might just be a couple of clouds. The bright, blue sky will always be there behind the clouds, which is the nature of Buddhism. When you can make it a practice to notice your emotions and thoughts daily, you are more aware of being a 'Watcher' and tap into our eternal dimension of pure consciousness.

- Make Compassion and Kindness a Priority

Doing your best to be more compassionate and kind shows the teachings of Buddha. Every living thing deserves to be treated kindly, and you need to make this kind of behavior a priority if you want to embody Buddhism. Wearing jewelry like a pendant or bracelet that is a symbol of Buddhism can help you remember to practice compassion and kindness during your day.

- Meditate Daily

Meditation is the backbone of Buddhism and the most powerful gateway to finding higher consciousness. But it does take some time and discipline to reap its rewards. Committing to sitting still for meditation is the most valuable way to live a life of Buddhism. Think about making a Zen garden or altar to be the space where you meditate.

SETTING UP YOUR DAILY PRACTICE

Begin your morning by saying your mantras. Build up to daily motivation by saying various prayers or by reading the Bodicitta mindfulness or Bodhisattva attitude.

You could also practice *Guru Shakyamuni Guru Yoga, Guru Puja,* or *Lama Tsongkhapa Guru Yoga*. While you are doing your yoga, you can meditate. It doesn't matter if you have been given a specific number of prostrations; it would be great if you could do between 35 and 100 prostrations by saying the "35 Buddhas of Confession."

Before you go to sleep, you are supposed to say one of the Vajrasattva mantras 21 times or a short one 28 times while meditating on the four opposing powers. By doing this, you will have a perfect confession.

When you get to the end, make an extensive dedicated prayer by using one of these: *"Blissful Realm Prayer," "Maitreya Buddha Prayer," "Shantideva's Guide to the Bodhisattva's Way of Life," "Middle and End," "Lama Tsongkhapa's Beginning," "The King of Prayers."*

You can also start to add in your own things that you find meaningful and gradually work your way through your own special practice.

MORE PRACTICES THAT YOU COULD DO

- Prostrate Yourself to the 35 Buddhas Each Morning

BUDDHISM

If at all possible, you should prostrate and recite the 35 Buddha's Confession three times every day. That comes out to 105 prostrations.

If you really think about this, you will understand the reasons why this should be done. Reciting all the Buddhas' names will bring your mind away from your negative karma from the past and purify the karma. If you don't take the time to cleanse the negative karma, you aren't going to get a good rebirth with the ten richnesses and eight freedoms that you have. You will experience the total opposite and be reborn into suffering within one of the lower realms. Plus, if this negative karma is left uncleaned, you will increase it in your mind. This is why it is so important to get it cleaned.

The reason you need to express these 35 Buddha's' existence is to understand that sentient beings have the ability to purify all types of negative karma that you may have picked up throughout your lives. Just saying the names of all the Buddhas just one time will purify all the most of your negative karma. It is similar to the way an atomic bomb works, meaning it can powerfully and quickly destroy all negative karma.

Lama Tsong Khapa did over 1000 prostrations while confessing to the 35 Buddhas while living in his cave at Olka, Tibet. The Lama Atisha did several prostrations daily, even when he was old, just like some of the other lam-rim lamas. Because of this, they were able to achieve several realizations.

. . .

This means you should practice the 35 Buddhas daily as it is an essential ingredient in your life as a Buddhist. If you want to be a healthy Buddhist, this is the best thing that you can do.

- Nightly Recite the Vajrasattva

While you are getting ready for bed every night, you need to recite the Vajrassattva mantra to keep all the negative karma that could have accumulated during your day from growing. If you don't take the time to cleanse it through this process, that karma is going to keep growing daily, weekly, monthly, and yearly until you die. A single day of negative karma can be as heavy as a mountain, and over time, even a tiny little atom of negative karma could grow to be the same size as the entire world.

Although you might not have created a lot of negative karma, uncleansed negative karma can increase at an exponential rate. One tiny bit could mean that you get reborn in a lower realm. This will cause you to suffer for many thousands of years. When you are in the lower realms, you will constantly be creating more and more negative karma; it will be very hard to get reborn into the upper realms. This is why you can practice Dharma every day. This is the reason you have to cleanse your negative karma daily.

Cleansing negative karma makes it easier to find the path to enlightenment and achieve liberation. It can get rid of any obstacles that might come up along with your suffering. When you cleanse your negative karma, you aren't going to have to experience the thousands of years of suffering inside the lower realms.

You have to cleanse all delusions and obstacles to see the realizations while journeying down the path toward enlightenment, so your work will be perfect for all the sentient beings. You won't bring them any temporary happiness but bring them liberation from samsara and ultimate happiness so that they won't ever experience sufferings again and help you reach enlightenment. Reaching enlightenment means you have to get rid of all the tiny mistakes in your mind and totally reach your realizations. By doing this, we can cleanse our life's problems like health and relationship problems that came from negative karma. Disasters happen because of negative karma. Because negative karma can be cleaned in this way, there is no need to experience health problems or catastrophes like cancer, but if you do, these are usually very minor.

All of this depends on the way you practice your purification. If you can practice your purification perfectly, continuously, and strongly, this means your being will be free of suffering.

Basically, even though you might have finished reciting all the thousands of Vajrasattva mantras, you can't just say: "I have finished my Vajrasattva preliminary, and now I don't have to recite that mantra anymore." You will have to recite that long mantra 21 times or say the short one 28 times daily to keep cleansing your negative karma so it won't multiply.

- Medicine Buddha Mantra

You can recite the Medicine Buddha mantra to help you reach success. Because you might have a lot of problems, but you want to succeed, you are going to want to say the Medicine Buddha mantra daily. This can help you get rid of suffering, problems you don't want or need, and unhappiness. It will allow you to gain the inner growth, realizations, happiness, and success you need.

Buddha informed Ananda, an attendant, that animals who heard this mantra couldn't be born into a lower realm. Kyabje Choden Rinpoche, who reached enlightenment, explained that those who recited this mantra while dying would be reborn in the pure land. Therefore, reciting this will not only help you heal, but it will benefit animals and people, whether dying or living.

When you say this each day, you can cleanse negative karma, which will prevent you from getting born into a lower realm. If your karma doesn't get cleanses, once you die, you will likely find yourself born into a lower realm as either a hungry ghost or an animal, and you are going to experience suffering time and time again. This is the main reason why you have to cleanse your negative karma immediately. Suppose you can't handle suffering now on this level, which could be considered joy compared to the lower realms' suffering. How are you going to be able to handle the intense suffering inside the lower realms, which is completely unbearable and lasts for a very long time and will be worse than any suffering you have endured up to this point.

• • •

*B*ecause saying the Medicine Buddha mantra can save you from suffering, it might be a lot more valuable to you than jewels, diamonds, gold, and countless money. Material wealth means nothing since it doesn't cleanse your karma. Even if you were the richest person in the world, just hearing or say this mantra a single time would be more valuable since it will imprint the path to enlightenment into your mind, get rid of all your subtle and gross defilements, help you gain the realizations along the path, and help you reach enlightenment.

This mantra could help you free many sentient beings from their suffering and help them reach enlightenment, so you have to make sure that you say it with truth, knowing that Buddha can take care of you, heal you, and be with you. Buddha resides with the crown chakra, heart chakra, or right in front of you. There is not a moment in your life where Medicine Buddha won't see you or have compassion.

- Reciting The Chrnrezig Mantra

*A*ll students need to practice the Compassionate Eye Looking One. Meditating while reciting this mantra can bring happiness to you and countless sentient beings. Saying this mantra can bring numerous benefits, especially if you do it along with the Bodhicitta.

*P*racticing and realizing the Bodhicitta is one important thing you can do for your life since it fulfills your wishes for happiness but to other sentient beings. When adding it to the Bodhicitta, you can rid yourself of an entire ocean of suffering and can bring freedom and enlightenment since it can help you gain wisdom to realize all the emptiness that can eradicate both the subtle and gross defilements.

Bodhicitta lets Arya Bodhisattvas let go of all the sufferings of samsara, and this includes death, sickness, old age, and rebirth just by finding the right-seeing path. Although arhats come from fewer paths, they have the knowledge to realize emptiness and other qualities, and they have the other aggregates of suffering.

Bodhicitta is the way in which you can reach the Mahayana path that will lead you to enlightenment. It is the root of Buddha's mind, speech, and holy body. The Bodhisattvas can bear every hardship for all the sentient beings, and it doesn't matter their size or if they die. Bodhisattvas can see the benefit of bearing other people's hardships; it helps them experience limitless joy. For a Bodhisattvas, dying for another person is like drinking the nectar of the gods, and in doing so, they experience the delightfulness of jumping into a cool pool on a hot day.

Bodhisattvas let go of thinking about reaching their own freedom from suffering and its cause, just like one throws away a used piece of tissue. They only have an aversion to gaining enlightenment for themselves.

Bodhicitta lets Bodhisattvas finish reaching two merits: virtue and wisdom. This is the main reason they try to achieve the two holy bodies or dharmakaya and rupakaya. The main reason they want to achieve these two bodies is so they can perform perfect works for every sentient being. While a lot of sentient beings are out there, it may take three eons to finish this accumulation so everyone can be enlightened. The thing that gives the Bodhisattvas their determination to do this is the Bodhicitta.

It doesn't matter how long it takes them to have one virtue, though; the Bodhisattva is going to always try to make it happen. Maitreya said: "In order to ripen even one virtuous thought, the Bodhisattva, the child of the Victorious Ones whose mind is stabilized in supreme perseverance for highly ripening the sentient beings, does not get discouraged, even if it takes thousands of ten million eons."

It is easy to see the determination that pushed Bodhisattvas to bear all of the numerous hardships and works constantly for sentient beings originates from the Bodhicitta. This is due to their compassion. Compassion helps to fuel the benefits of the Bodhicitta, just like jet fuel-powered airplanes or electricity generated by a power plant can light up a whole city.

This compassion is what has brought sentient beings to enlightenment and will continue to help bring more sentient beings to enlightenment. Having a lot of compassion is what helps Buddhas do amazing work for the sentient beings once they reach enlightenment. This great compassion makes all Buddhas have a perfect power and an omniscient mind that they need to help every sentient being.

. . .

Your own compassion becomes a source of happiness and peace for numerous sentient beings. It is their source for ultimate and temporary happiness, and this includes the beings in this world like your children, companion, parents, and yourself.

If you don't have compassion in your heart and the only thing in your heart is ego, this will harm every sentient being, including the ones in the world, along with your children, companion, parents, and yourself. The more you practice compassion, the more happiness and peace will live in your life and heart.

If you want to develop great compassion, you are going to need to understand Buddha's teaching and ways you can develop them. Even if you do recite all of the teachings about compassion and know them by heart, and understand how to meditate on them, this won't be enough for you to realize it. To accomplish this, you will need to support all of the blessings of Avalokiteshvara, or as he is most commonly known, the Buddha of Compassion. If you are looking to receive these types of blessings, you have to practice reciting this mantra along with meditating.

- Recite the *"Golden Light Sutra"* To Achieve World Peace

If you are looking to create world peace, then the Gold Light Sutra is what you will want to read. This is extremely important if you want to stop all the wars and violence within the world today. This mantra is the best one to bring about world peace. Everybody can do this, no matter how busy they may be or even what religion they follow. You may choose only to read one page or a few lines each, but if you can do this constantly, you will make it to the end of the sutra.

This is the king of all the sutras. It has extreme powers, can fulfill every wish, and can bring peace and happiness to every sentient being, too. It is very powerful in helping promote world peace while also helping to protect yourself, your county, and the world as a whole. It also holds the power to heal people within a country.

For those looking to find peace for themselves and others, Dharma is a great way to find that peace in ways that won't need harm, criticizing, or demonstrating against anyone else. All you have to do is read it, and you will find peace. There is no need to be Buddhist to read the sutra and find peace. People who aren't Buddhists but want peace can read it to have some good effects.

This sutra can protect countries and people from natural disasters. These events aren't natural since they come from the right conditions and causes.

This means you can't measure the benefits of reading the sutra. It has been said that a person creates more merit by saying a couple of the lines of this sutra than if they made offerings to Buddha of every precious jewel that equals the pieces of sand in the Atlantic Ocean.

STARTING YOUR JOURNEY

These are the basics of Buddhism, but it could take years to meditate and study to get familiar with Buddhism. If you want Buddhism to be a part of your life, you just need to begin exploring and finding your own way. There isn't a wrong or right way; your journey depends totally on you.

CONCLUSION

Thank you for making it through to the end of the book; let's hope it was informative and able to provide you with all of the tools you need to achieve your goals, whatever they may be.

Whether you chose this book for educational purposes or you're thinking about following the Buddhist faith, I hope you enjoyed every part of it. As you move forward in your beliefs and life, do so consciously. If Buddha's teachings feel right to you, then Buddhism may be the right path for you. If you find that it doesn't resonate well, that's okay as well. Do what you feel is going to benefit you the most. Even if you don't feel like becoming a Buddhist, you can use some of their practices to bring more peace into your life.

DEB LILITH

5 ESSENTIAL MINDFUL HABITS

Copyright © 2020 by Deb Lilith

All rights reserved.

No part of this book may be reproduced in any form or by any electronic or mechanical means, including information storage and retrieval systems, without written permission from the author, except for the use of brief quotations in a book review.

INTRODUCTION

I want to thank you and congratulate you for downloading the book "*The Five Essential Mindfulness Habits.*"

This book contains proven steps and strategies for building mindfulness habits and finding peace in your life. The reality is, we are living in a world that runs on autopilot and survival mode. These two modes of living do *not* contribute to the happy and joyous lives we desire to lead. We follow false promises that making significant income figures, working hard, and doing everything we are "supposed" to do will bring us the joy and peace we desire. The truth of it is, they won't. Only you have the power to do that.

Once you take control of your own life and begin implementing habits that lead to a happy and positive life right now, everything in your life changes. You will no longer be waiting for individual circumstances to be met for you to experience the life you desire. You will no longer feel as though you are always chasing something that you aren't even sure exists. You will no longer feel like you are still just around the corner from everything you've ever wanted. Instead, you will feel as though you are officially

INTRODUCTION

commanding your own experience right now and that everything else that happens for you, now and in the future, is all just evidence of your peaceful and joyous existence here on Earth.

The more you practice the mindfulness habits, the more you gain control over your thoughts. You start feeling calmer and develop patience. It makes you more joyous, playful, and able to spend quality time with family and friends.

This book will prove to be your primer for mindfulness. Every effort was made to ensure this book is full of as much useful information as possible. Please enjoy!

WHAT IS MINDFULNESS?

MINDFULNESS TAKES its roots in Buddhist meditation, but this practice has entered the American mainstream in recent years. Mindfulness is the essential human ability to be present at the moment, be fully aware of our actions and surroundings, and react without judgment on what's going on inside and around us.

To be mindful means maintaining a moment-by-moment awareness of your feelings, bodily sensations, thoughts, and surrounding. When you continuously become aware of what you are experiencing using the senses, or the mind, you are mindful. It is also about releasing yourself from making a judgment. When you get into the habit of paying more attention to your thoughts and emotions, you develop a neutral stand towards yourself and others. You become more impartial in processing information, so you stop being biased and subjective.

Thanks to research, mindfulness is not just a New Age technique that only a handful of people know about. It's now a practice that millions of people around the world have. Mindfulness has the power to transform your life, but only if you allow it. Taking hold of your life and using mindfulness as a tool is a decision you need to make yourself. The good thing about this journey is that you don't need to take any drastic action to change your life. At this point, you just need to make a choice and stick to it.

In simple terms, mindfulness is the ability to be present in the here and now and be conscious and aware at the moment. It is the ability to be in the present moment and be fully engaged without distractions without letting your mind wander to the past or future.

It is a mental state that you achieve by focusing your awareness on the present. Often used as a form of therapy to help patients become aware of the present moment while gently acknowledging their feelings and thoughts, mindfulness helps you grow significantly in self-awareness without judgment.

The human mind has a lot of thoughts daily. When you add stress and the complexity of life to a person's daily lifestyle, your mind can go haywire due to pressure, anxiety, stress, and depression. Even simple thoughts can become too repetitive and obsessive, draining your energy, focus and causing mental confusion and fear. Mindfulness practice can help teach you how to direct your attention from chaotic or repetitive thinking to a calm and clear focus.

Mindfulness is known to engage the human body's relaxation response, where the parasympathetic nervous system becomes engaged. This system usually kicks in after you have experienced stress and responded to it. It helps your body calm down, decreasing your heart rate, respiratory rate, the tension in your muscles, blood pressure, and lowering your heightened awareness during stress to relax. Mindfulness helps induce this response more quickly, thus allowing both your mind and your body to relax.

· · ·

Why is this Popular Now?

Mindfulness has grown in popularity in the last decade, particularly as awareness of this healthy practice has become mainstream. Many psychologists, therapists, and doctors have embraced this healthy practice as clinical studies have proven how mindfulness practice can improve health and longevity. It also helps patients increase their self-awareness, gain self-control, drop unhealthy addictive habits, and develop a more positive outlook in life.

Mindfulness practice is also widespread today among many working professionals who experience a lot of pressure at work and face burnout. Burnout can create physical exhaustion, emotional exhaustion, feelings of deep anxiety, insomnia, chest pains, depression, alienation, and give rise to deep-seated fears of inadequacy. When working professionals feel too much pressure, they may also think they are not accomplishing enough at work, which leads to depression and withdrawal despite their best efforts at the time.

While physical pain is the most visible sign of distress, human beings may also experience mental torture and suffering that go unaddressed quietly until they have a breakdown.

Mindfulness practice has become a way for you to improve your life right away by reducing stress and developing internal tranquility to reboot your way of thinking essentially. Mindfulness practice is most often done through meditation, which offers you a way to pause and relax, reducing your stress immediately.

Mindfulness has its roots in ancient meditation practices in India and south-central Asia. Ayurveda is an ancient medical practice in India that recognizes mindfulness as part of a healthy body-mind connection. *Prana,* or life energy, is considered essential to healthy functioning. Through mindfulness practice, a person can learn to direct this energy and learn how to focus your attention. This Eastern practice recognizes the synergy between the body and mind. Today Western practitioners have adopted this practice to heal the mind and body and to promote wellbeing. Regular mindfulness practice has been known to improve one's quality of life.

How to make mindfulness a habit

Creating a routine for one to follow is essential. A practice tells you what to do. It is a guideline of what is expected of you to do in order to achieve something. It helps one to track all activities and to know what is next. Since mindfulness takes time to be fully incorporated by a person, a routine helps to give that daily groove. So, the routine works as an assistant in the journey to have and find the way to being mindful.

Another thing is setting reasonable goals. For one to find their way to be mindful, then one has to set goals. What do reasonable goals mean? Reasonable goals mean those goals that are easy and more likely to be followed by one. One must set goals that he or she can reach. They must not be exaggerated since if they are, one will not achieve whatever they wanted to. To match his or her expectations, they must set reasonable and customary goals for that to happen. When goals are valid, then the results are great too.

Being consistent is also very important. It is essential since one has to follow one's plan of action for one to achieve something. It is easy since all one has to do is follow their everyday routine and look up to their goals to help them through. Consistency helps to keep things smooth and flawless. They help keep things in check and keep things moving towards one's goals, dreams, and desires. It keeps things going at any time despite the things that come up or the hiccups that come up.

Appreciating oneself every time is another crucial thing to do. It is called patting someone on the back. When someone appreciates themselves, it makes them very happy and also confident. This confidence helps one to go for their goals. Being appreciative is something that everyone should master and keep so that they can improve on their self-confidence. Everything that one does good, he or she must appreciate, which helps one be better at everything one does. It is because of the increased self-positivism and also confidence. The appreciation of everyone is significant and essential to everyone too.

Mindfulness keeps things in check in all social systems. Mindfulness has a lot of benefits to a person and also the people around him. The benefits are very positive and have a lot of beneficial characters that come with it. One learns patience, self-awareness, clarity of the mind. Mindfulness keeps a person sane and happy. It also enables a person to be focused and well-rested. It also allows one to improve the things that happen in his or her life. It enables one to remove negative thoughts and replace them with positive ones in one's life.

MINDFUL EATING

MINDFUL EATING IS DEFINED as the idea of having an open mind and being aware that any food eaten has its effect on the body. Has effects also on the mind and what surrounds it. When food is eaten mindfully, it is enjoyed every bit and engages all senses to appreciate the body. Mindful eating also focuses on the fact that individuals are aware of the food they eat and the experience they have from it.

Mindful eating is also the ability to be aware that there are positive opportunities made available from the food selected. It helps to do away with any distractions and enjoy food. It is the ability to take time over any meal, understanding that eating more and slowly is advisable. It gives the ability to enjoy the meal, the aromas, and the different textures. And hence one can have a reconnection with their senses. When the process is experienced, there is the enjoyment and pleasure of eating.

. . .

It gives the ability to wisely choosing what we eat, satisfying our taste buds, and getting body nourishment—responding to the different foods, what they like or dislike without judging anything—becoming aware of being physically hungry and when to decide and eat. Eating mindfully involves several aspects. There are different ways of creating awareness of the food experience. Some of the primary measures of freedom of eating can be achieved through statements such as:

- That there are no right or bad eating habits
- Everyone has their unique eating habits
- Ensure there is adherence to eating moment by moment
- Knowing about the connection between living beings and the Earth
- There is a need to promote balance, wisdom, acceptance, and choices.

There are many people out there who struggle with food and also their thoughts and feelings. It is the reason why people do mindless eating and repeat their past actions while feeling very powerless to change their lives.

Mindfulness eating does increase the awareness of your mind regarding your destructive eating patterns without being judgmental; thus, it helps create space between your actions and your craving triggers. Below are the benefits of mindful eating:

Increased enjoyment of food: Mindful eating allows you to find new respect for your food; thus, you gain more pleasure from eating your meals.

Reduced likelihood of overeating: Overeating is a common social problem in many societies, leading to different health problems. Mindful eating allows you to reduce your cravings, so you don't overeat to not suffer from lifestyle diseases.

Being full while eating less: Mindful eating can also help you feel full while eating less. Since you don't let your feelings and emotions get to you, you remove your cravings while eating, so instead of chowing down a whole chocolate cake, you will be more satisfied with one or two slices of cake with mindful eating.

Improves digestion: Contrary to what most people think, digestion does not start in the stomach. In reality, digestion begins in the mouth with saliva's action breaking down the starch in food. Mindful eating allows you to improve your digestion because you eat your food slowly and more carefully

Now that you already know the basics and benefits of mindful eating, it is time that you practice mindful eating. Practicing mindful eating can be challenging, especially if you have been mindless eating for many years. Thus, this section will give you tips on how to practice mindful eating.

Practicing mindful eating for the first time is tough, but you need to train yourself hard. Preparing yourself for mindful eating requires you to ask yourself important questions. The questions are similar to the "Am I hungry?"

Below are tips on how to do self-help practice for mindful eating.

Determine why you want to eat now

Before you take a bite of your food, determine the reason why you want to eat. Are you physically hungry, or are you just bored or emotionally distressed? So instead of mindless putting food in your mouth, wait and think first. Give yourself time or have a glass of water. If you think about it, you might not be starving at all.

Determine what you want to eat

When hungry, do not just grab the food nearest you. Determine what food you want to eat. Ask yourself if you want something salty or sweet. Once you start to find out the type of food you want to eat, you end up eating in smaller amounts; thus, you don't binge eat. If you find out what your food preferences are, you are less inclined to eat more.

Determine how much enjoyment you are getting from your food

Once you start eating, pay attention to the flavor, texture, and scent of your food. Ask yourself how much enjoyment you get from food. For this process, you need at least 20 minutes for the brain to process the messages from your stomach. As you chew your food, think about how much satisfaction you get on a scale of 1 to 10. If you do this, you will realize that your enjoyment does not rely on food.

Determine how full you are

If you eat fast and mindlessly, you end up eating past the point of being genuinely full. When eating, pay attention to how full you feel. You can also rate your satiation level on a scale of 1 to 10.

Determine why you ate how much of a particular type of food

Part of mindful eating is learning from your mistakes. While it is easy to memorize mindful eating principles, following them to the hilt is very difficult. So next time when you go a little crazy over ice cream, ask yourself why you ate a certain amount of it. It is related to your emotions, and maybe you can avoid overeating next time if you deal with the feelings related to your binge eating.

MINDFUL BREATHING

BREATHING IS A GIFT OF LIFE; it is the breath of life that accompanies us day by day. Breathing with awareness gives us the ability to live in harmony and enjoy the present moment. The present moment is the only moment that is real.

When we breathe consciously, we can extract the vital energy from the oxygen we breathe, thus filling ourselves with health, energy, and vitality. Breathing nourishes us, heals us, helps us expand our perception, and sees the world differently.

Long, deep, conscious breathing gives us calm and enables us to make correct decisions. Short, shallow breathing causes anxiety, stress, fear, and other negative emotions.

Breathing with awareness allows us to think correctly — because the mind always follows the breath — speak correctly, feel correct, act rightly, and have a positive mental attitude.

Every breath we take with awareness can reduce stress and anxiety levels to which we are subjected by excess information. Breathing with understanding can bring us calm, security, health, success, and prosperity. It also helps us control our thoughts, emotions, feelings and supports us to have control of our physical body.

Breathing with awareness helps us to be neutral and to live in peace with ourselves and our environment. Breathing with conscience makes us better people every day. In the breath is the secret of our happiness, health, success, and prosperity.

Mindful breathing means that you focus entirely on your breath as you breathe, so you become more aware of it. Breathing is vital for our survival. However, it is something we take for granted, mainly because it occurs involuntarily. It is why we fail to recognize it or improve it.

You may not know that most of us have the habit of taking shallow breaths and studies show that shallow breathing is one of the significant triggers of anxiety. If you live in a state of anxiousness all the time, you find it difficult to focus on the present and be mindful of it. To become more aware of the moment and to save yourself from the harms of anxiety, start breathing mindfully. Yes, conscious breathing can easily curb your anxiety and save you from succumbing to depression now and then. Since it trains you to be more aware of your breath, it helps you cultivate a present consciousness, which keeps you from falling prey to anxiety and depression triggering thoughts.

Mindful breathing is an exercise that you can do anytime, any place. As long as you have a few moments to tune into your breath, you will be able to fulfill this practice. The benefit of mindful breathing is that it grounds you to your body and brings your awareness back to the present moment. As humans, we tend to get wrapped up in the stresses and worries that bog down our minds. We are likely to find ourselves trapped in intrusive thought patterns that tie us to the past or get us too concerned about strange events that may or may not happen in the future.

When we find ourselves in this state of being trapped within our minds and not gaining any value from our thoughts, we must learn to consciously send our awareness elsewhere in our body: such as to our breath. It allows us to take our conscious focus away from the problematic area, reconnect with our bodies, center ourselves, and rediscover what matters. Similar to the "Counting to 10" practice that we often teach kids, connecting to our breath in this way gives us time to calm down and gain some perspective when it is needed the most. You can use this practice any time that you feel that you are trapped within your mind. Whether you are dealing with intrusive thoughts, outdated or outgrown thought patterns, anxiety, stress, sadness, or anything else you are struggling with, this practice can help you.

Mindful breathing is a powerful exercise for one huge reason: when we slow down our breath, we slow down our stress. If you think about it, any time you become stressed or unhappy with something, your breath likely shallows and quickens. By intentionally deepening your breath, you allow yourself to slow down your thoughts and reduce the instance of negative and stressful emotions. You give yourself back your self-control. We breathe all the time involuntarily.

Mindful breathing involves our conscious participation in the breathing process. It's beyond the general practice of the inhalation and exhalation of the air. It demands more focus and attention towards every breathe we take in. It can be carried out at any time of the day. But to do so, make sure that you are at a place where plenty of fresh air is available. This place should also be isolated so that nobody could disturb you during the process. It is carried out simultaneously with meditation most of the time. After selecting a suitable time and place, you should think about how you want to breathe by standing or sitting down. If you can't find a place to sit, then it can be practiced while standing, but the ideal position is to sit and make yourself comfortable first.

Steps to Mindful Breathing

Mindful breathing is most effective when practiced during panic attacks or stressful conditions. It helps in regaining sense and the much-needed calm. There are a few necessary steps of mindful breathing.

At first, take a deep breath through your nostrils for three seconds.

Now, hold your breath for about two seconds to allow the absorption of the oxygen.

Now, open your mouth and exhale through it slowly in four seconds.

These three steps seem pretty simple and easy, but when you repeat the same steps in continuity, there are chances of getting distracted or being caught up in the thoughts. Therefore, it is crucial to continually remind yourself that you are exercising your breath and not sitting idle. With this idea in mind, you might be able to stick to the practice. Do not prolong the breathing session if you cannot maintain your concentration. Start with five minutes a day, and when you master this practice, increase the time to 10 and then 15 minutes in a day. The only condition is to stay in the moment and focus on your breathing. Feel yourself taking all that air into your lungs and coming out of it. Be aware of your breathing and then see the difference.

Comfort is essential when you are practicing mindfulness. If you are sitting in an uncomfortable environment or a place, it will disrupt your whole experience and not guarantee good results. Select a pure and noiseless location for this practice. Do not push yourself to inhale more than your built capacity; inhale as much as you can, then focus on exhaling. Know your limits and then set your breathing according to them. Select an appropriate schedule as per your routine, rate of metabolism, body type, mental potential, and illnesses (if any). If you are suffering from any lung-related disease, it is recommended to consult your doctor first before trying these steps.

EXPRESSING GRATITUDE

MINDFULNESS GRATITUDE MEANS to be aware of your blessings in every moment that you experience so you can pay your appreciation of the universe for them and cultivate thankfulness.

Gratitude is an important habit to develop because it helps you become more aware of your blessings and live in the moment. When you aren't mindful of your gifts, you will likely ignore your present and whine about things you don't have, and even worry incessantly about your future. This habit makes you hate your life and increase your stress. If you want to escape all of this and manifest a better life, you must build a nurturing gratitude tradition.

When you take a moment to experience the things that you are grateful for as if they were unfolding right before you, you become better aware of them and relish the happiness you experience then for a long time. For instance, if you are grateful for the way your loved one kissed your forehead in the morning, remember it as it happened – as if you can feel their lips touching your skin.

You live the life you own for yourself. It is the person's option of how he will make through all the curses and blessings. We all know that there are lines with soft flowers and so is the case with life; so instead of being jealous of others or creating problems for yourself by being lustful, try to fascinate your very own self by every step you take. You should become your ideal. What is the thing that makes you wonder a person's life? It is only the satisfaction that comes to their forehead hiding the frowns of worldly tensions. Nobody ever has fantasized a billionaire on a death bed with several shitty problems? But can you figure out the reason? It is just a lack of satisfaction though he had a lot of money.

By all of this, we got to know that satisfaction is the key to happiness and idealism. The roots of satisfaction adhere to gratitude. Gratitude is the satisfaction you have with yourself, your life, your standards and your demands. It is just the thinking that what I have is the best for me; to be content with what one has and be grateful in every breath. You will meet several people in your life, some of which you would find fine-looking and some with a subtle pocket; maybe you would lack in front of some, but the thing that would be your strength is the gratitude you possess. Their wealth or looks or background cannot let you down by this very trait of yours.

You must know that gratitude leads to real success in life. It specifically makes a person so much independent in thoughts that he can speak out and be opinionative. We have many people around us who have nothing special but still are the centre point of everyone's attention. Have you ever thought about this? Its mere reason is the confidence they hold due to their gratitude nature. When a person is grateful for whatever he has, he gets fearless and confident. He, then, holds the guts to confront the worst situations and to lead them with honour.

It is hell essential to understand that what you have got is the best for you and that nobody else can have it as you have. So instead of being insecure, rejoice the moments of love and be merry.

Accept it if you feel scared or shy and try to get in touch with your inner soul. Linger over your feelings and ponder over the way you feel and the sensations you go through. Only you can stop this. Have faith in yourself. You should never feel inferior to anyone, own yourself. You see, the thought that only other people have a right to speak is wrong. You should communicate. It is the key to overcoming your shyness. Talk out your heart; sing a song with your newly made friends. It helps you connect with each and reduce any form of hesitation if it exists. Just rub it away from your soul.

To practice mindfulness-based gratitude, do the following.

Give Thanks before Having a Meal

Often, when food is placed before us, we are either too hungry or so much in a hurry, we shove the food in our mouths without being thankful. We forget that not everyone has had the chance to have such a meal.

Giving thanks before a meal recognizes all the hard work of the people who made it possible for you to have food on your table. For the religious, you thank God for the blessing of a meal. Whatever it is, it is just a moment to pause and be mindful, appreciate, and feel blessed that you have the food and nourishment you need. Here are some gratitude words you can use;

- *(Dear Lord)*

We are about to eat for the meal for everyone that made it possible, and for those, we can share it with, we are grateful.

You can also be creative and write your own. Just make it short and straightforward, so you do not dread saying it when hunger is gnawing.

Morning Coffee/Tea Gratitude

There is no better way to start your morning than being grateful. The best thing is that you do not have to be just seated in meditation to be thankful. In any case, most of us will claim that we do not have the time. To ensure you don't miss opportunities to be grateful, you can tie your gratitude sessions with your morning coffee/tea!

With your coffee in hand, sit back and think of the things that you are thankful for. They could be as simple as:

- The aroma of the coffee
- The warmth of the coffee mug in hand
- The bright and beautiful morning
- The sensation of the warm drink going into your body
- The beginning of a new day, a fresh opportunity to live

Gratitude Stroll

If you are not one of those who go for morning runs for fitness, you can take a walk to make a gratitude stroll. You don't need to follow a track or road. Just go for a walk to see just how many positive things you can find; you may find yourself wandering through some grass or shrubs (be sure that it's safe, though).

Some of these things could be wildflowers or flowers growing in unlikely places, such as a window sill, a cloudless sky, or the smell of pancakes, bread, and other breakfast delicacies in the neighborhood. Appreciate that you can see and feel these things.

Gratitude Journal

Keep a gratitude journal in which you can write down a few things that you are grateful for. You can do this in the morning or the evening (to finish your day strong as it will impact your morning). In the morning, write down the things that you are grateful for. For instance, you are healthy, your family is happy, your children burst into your bedroom to kiss you good morning, and so on.

In the evening, write down five things about your day for which you are grateful. Notice that, some days you will have exciting things to write and others just the simple things that go unnoticed quite often. It is not only exciting things that should be reported. It is the simple ones you should be keen to notice. For instance, getting home safe is something to be thankful for. This way, there will never be a day that is too bad that there is nothing to be grateful for.

Gratitude Lookout

Look out for things (even if they cannot answer/hear you) and people to thank right from when you wake up.

For instance, thank the stove for helping you make breakfast without burning you, thank the towel for drying you so correctly, and thank the car for starting up with no hitches.

As for people, you can start with those around you when you wake up. Actively watch out for people that are helpful, kind, or considerate. It will save you from the bad habit of entitlement. For instance, thank your spouse for doing something as little as zipping your dress or ironing your shirt. Thank them for loving you and just being there. Say thank you when your child, sibling, or friend passes the juice at breakfast and so on.

Gratitude through the Eyes of Another

We all have things that we once appreciated but now seem ordinary to us – we start taking them for granted. You can rekindle the appreciation by seeing these things through the eyes of another. You can do the following with a friend:

- Let them listen to a collection of music that you have created
- Introduce them to your significant other
- Let them spent the weekend at your home
- Invite them to share dinner that your significant other made
- Take them to see your favorite movie.

CONSCIOUS OBSERVATION

~~~~

ANOTHER USEFUL MINDFULNESS habit is Observation. It is about just noticing the present rather than thinking about the present. In this habit, you allow your direct experience to happen – without labeling what is happening or trying to change it.

Observation can be directed inward and outward. Inward Observation means to become aware of your feelings, breath, body sensations, and thoughts without judging it. Outward Observation includes noticing what you sense from outside, seeing, tasting, touching, and hearing without reacting to it or labeling it.

Mindful Observation can help you to stop auto-pilot behavior and check-in with what is going on right now. By checking in with what you feel, you can make better decisions about what is right for you right now. By checking in with your thoughts, you can make choices based on what matters to you. By checking in with your sensations, you can notice when you need rest. By checking in the circumstances, you can get a more clear vision of the situation.

Observation can help you feel fully present in the moment and experience reality as it is. When you practice Observation, you are much more likely to be calm, centered, and aware. Observe in the shower or when eating your breakfast. Observe walking to your car and when driving to work. Observe at your workplace and the gym. The more you use it, the more aware and present you'll be.

However, if you observe things mindfully, it is likely that you won't make too much meaning of that encounter and won't perceive it as something negative. Instead of perceiving it as your best friend meeting with your ex-spouse and thinking they may be plotting something against you, you are likely to see them as two individuals who have a right to live freely meeting each other. When you start observing things mindfully, you keep your mind from falling into the traps of stress, anxiety, and depression and help it live in the moment and savor it. It enables you to feel happy, calm, and relaxed.

If you want to be a more mindful observer, try the following practice.

- Pick any natural object you would like to observe, such as a flower, a leaf, or a tree.
- Breathe mindfully for a few moments to re-center yourself and then start observing that chosen object.
- Pay attention to every tiny detail of that object and observe

it. If you are watching a tree, observe its bark, and see how thick or thin it is. Slowly move towards the branches and then the leaves and notice as many details as you can about every tiny to big part of the tree.
- Keep observing the object mindfully for at least 5 minutes.

When you end this exercise, you'll have noticed many new things about that object that you previously used to see mindlessly. Not only that, but you'll also be more appreciative of it as well. Make sure to observe things mindfully for 5 to 10 minutes twice a day and slowly do it more often. In a couple of weeks, you'll have built the habit of observing most things and situations around you mindfully, which will increase your level of mindfulness and make you more peaceful than before.

MINDFUL MEDITATION

IN THE RELIGION OF BUDDHISM, there is a popular concept known as "Sati." Sati, translated literally into the English language, means "Mindful." Being mindful is an essential tenet of Buddhism, a religion known for leading a lifestyle free from all wants and desires. Buddhists believe that the abandonment of desire for material possessions allows one to experience life as it is meant to be shared truly. It allows one to look at the beauty of the world and the universe in which it is contained and genuinely appreciates it, something that is not possible when one's mind is clouded by desire.

Mindfulness Meditation follows this basic principle of Buddhism. It is similar to Primordial Sound Meditation in its origin if not in its methodology and practice. The similarity lies in its semi Buddhist origins, applied to a western philosophy of general health and wellbeing, all of which come together to form this distinct branch of meditation that focuses on the shedding of baseless lust and desire. Mindfulness Meditation, in many ways, contains the very best of both worlds, these respective worlds being those of the mystical Far East and the more practical West.

In essence, Mindfulness Meditation finds its roots in the Buddhist practice of vipassana meditation. Vipassana meditation is performed through mindfulness of one's breathing, first and foremost. It means that you must be aware of your breathing. As you breathe in full awareness of your body's functions, you must contemplate the impermanence of your existence. You must view all things unsubstantial without the presence of an entity beyond your concept of consciousness, impermanence, or the confines of the physical world that you call your home. It is essential in achieving physical enlightenment through the practice of vipassana meditation.

Mindfulness Meditation focuses on the breathing aspect of vipassana meditation. As the practitioner of Mindfulness Meditation breathes consciously, he is meant to focus on the activity of breathing, being mindful of just this single process. One of the essential benefits of Mindfulness Meditation is that it is an excellent way to handle stress. It is easiest to apply meditation techniques that one can find because it is practically just breathing in a controlled manner, and concentrating on this breathing, ignoring all other thoughts and emotions that enter your mind. It has been proven to help improve concentration as well, as the emptying of your mind in this manner allows you, after the meditative process has been completed, to focus on a single task with a clear head.

Mindfulness Meditation has been so effective in its goals as the techniques sparked the creation of an actual Mindfulness Movement in the first years of the 21st century. It kickstarted in many ways curated by a single individual by the name of John Kabat-Zinn. The mindfulness movement now encompasses several techniques beyond meditation, such as acceptance and cognitive therapies, stress reduction, and behavior therapies. The mindfulness movement now comprises an entire branch of alternative medicine thanks to the concrete evidence supporting its techniques' benefits.

Mindfulness meditation is not complicated, but it should be practiced carefully. By no means should you do the techniques you will learn automatically as if they were part of a routine program that you engage in out of obligation? With that being said, mindfulness meditation goes hand in hand with a state of increased awareness and awakening that allows for no superficiality. Remember that mindfulness teaches you how to escape any suffering or discomfort that may tinge your life.

The most comfortable form of mindfulness is achieved through sitting meditation. You undoubtedly know the classic position in which Buddha is depicted. You are not trying to imitate Buddha when practicing mindfulness, but attempting to find yourself and appreciate every moment of your own life. However, there was much wisdom in Buddha's words, and you should at least remember his words of wisdom: our source of suffering is running away from direct experience. Starting from his notion of absolute acceptance and harmony with the self and the universe, you can practice mindfulness by paying attention to each detail of knowledge as it arises in a completely non-judgmental way.

The following meditation techniques are relatively simple for beginners, and they focus on your body, breath, and thoughts.

First of all, you should try to situate your body in the right setting for meditation. If you can afford to have an entire room that is incredibly quiet and relaxing, filled with optimal light and color and allowing for no disturbance or disharmony, that is great. However, most of us cannot, and it's easier to find a corner of a 'normal' room where you arrange something like a small altar for this activity. Ideally, you should decorate that corner or room with pictures and objects that have sacred meanings to you one way or another. Make sure no distractions are around, only calming and subtly inspiring images on the walls. The best way to take care of this aspect is to get rid of the usual 'food for thought' that keeps you farther away from mindfulness: TV set, computer, internet, etc. During mindfulness meditation, you are supposed to get into the most profound communication with yourself and your honest thoughts and sensations.

As for the place you should use for sitting, you can use a comfortable chair or sit directly on the floor on a soft cushion or on a blanket. Ideally, more direct contact with 'the ground' is desirable. However, suppose for any objective reason, you would be uncomfortable sitting on the floor. In that case, you are, of course, free to sit on a chair or a bench, as that is not necessarily going to affect your meditation. It would help if you were careful about your 'meditation seat' stability: it shouldn't wiggle or produce any pressure/discomfort. Cross your legs in front of you and place your hands on your thighs or knees with palms facing downwards. Look gently in front of you, letting your gaze linger on the objects that you can find around. Don't try to focus too sharply; the idea is letting your eyes rest as naturally as possible on whatever is surrounding you. It doesn't have to be anything special: if you're facing your window, just look at the forms and contours of the clouds; if you're facing vegetation, let your senses revel in the colors and shapes; if you see houses in front of you, move your gaze gently over the objects without straying into what is not there (e.g., don't try to imagine what is inside or people who may inhabit them, only focus on what is visible to the eyes); if you have your walls in front of you, looks softly at the pictures you have on them, etc.

The next thing you have to do is keep your back straight but relaxed. Let your front be open, and gently hold your stare on what you can see in front of you for a few minutes in a row. If your mind wanders, gently take note of the objects' concrete features in front of you: remind yourself to come back in the present moment, right in the setting you are located in. Nevertheless, you shouldn't do this in a too forced way: don't judge yourself harshly for thinking about something else, don't reprimand yourself explicitly or indirectly by dwelling on any negative energy. Simply bring your thoughts back to what you can see and observe in front of you and try to notice as many details as you can about your environment. Remember: after all, *mindfulness* means experiencing the present moment to the fullest with your whole mind. It is not any kind of multi-directionality or divergence that will help you feel fulfilled and in harmony with the concrete world around you.

After taking in your environment for a few minutes (about 5 minutes would be ideal), you can now focus on your breath. Notice the rhythm of your natural breath without trying to change it. Just make sure you are incredibly aware of the 'movements' of your breath: inhale, exhale; do this consciously and attentively for a few minutes, as if being one with your breath, playing its very tune with your conscious mind in perfect harmony. Focus mentally on your breath as if it were a fine traceable thread that you can follow with your thoughts.

After you made sure you are in touch with your breath, try focusing on your body and any sensations you might experience. How does the pillow or blanket beneath you feel? Are you barefoot? Do you feel any cold or warm air? What are you wearing? How do your clothes feel? When your palms touch your thighs, what precise tactile impressions do you get? Can you sense any smell in your room? Ideally, you should burn some incense or candles to stimulate your senses. Can you feel any taste in your mouth? Perhaps you have just eaten something delicious, and you can still vaguely perceive the taste? Don't imagine anything, don't force yourself to create mentally what is not already in front of you and you. Remember: if you can feel it in your body and take it in via your five senses, it is real.

The next step is focusing on your thoughts. The bottom line is that having your thoughts wander and develop in a stream of consciousness on their own is a natural mental process, and you should accept it and treat it with tolerance without letting yourself be controlled or absorbed by it. The point is to become aware of this process and be the master over it. How can you do this? It's easy: just pay attention to the direction of your thoughts during your meditation exercise. If you think about the last film you watched, slowly push it out of your mind, since it belongs in the past. If you find yourself fantasizing about a vacation or your crush, bring your thoughts back to yourself gently and focus on what is in front of you in the present moment. The easiest way to do this is to get your thoughts from an immaterial reality at first to your breath. Once you 'caught' yourself dreaming of something unreal or lingering on the past, follow the flow of your breath naturally for a few minutes. This simple act will bring you back to your immediate reality, back into your sensations and physical environment.

This meditation exercise should be practiced for 10-15 minutes for starters. After you have learned how to gently control your thoughts and mind (think the strategy 'an iron hand in a silk glove' for this purpose), you are already an expert in mindful meditation. It means you shouldn't let yourself grow too used to what you can easily do. Instead, you should increase the duration of your exercise to 20-30 minutes. Eventually, this calming and healthy mindfulness exercise can extend up to 45 minutes. You will be able to decide on this aspect once you realize how beneficial and revitalizing it is.

The key to mindfulness meditation is getting a grip over your thoughts and being able to 'maneuver' yourself back into the delights of the present moment instead of longing for unreal worlds. There may be a preconception that mindfulness meditation could imply voiding the mind of your usual thought tracks and patterns, of your memories, etc. It couldn't be further from the truth. The goal of this practice is exercising control over your thoughts and avoiding stress or pain. When you have regularly swept away from the present into a fantasy world or recollections of past events, something may be wrong – are you delighted with what you already have? Are you even aware of what is tangible to you and graspable in front of you? Most of the time, when we neglect the joys of the present moment, we do it unknowingly because we may miss something or we simply lack practice. Through mindfulness meditation, you are intentionally training your mind via your own will.

CONCLUSION

Thank you for reading this book, and congratulations for reading until the end.

Success is not a big event; it is made up of little actions done every day. Prime your life by cultivating awareness in every little thing you do. Learn to appreciate the preciousness of a moment – be present to see it. Create that by practicing mindfulness.

Thank you, and good luck!